JESUS REVIVAL

RETURNING TO OUR FIRST LOVE

JAY MORGAN

APC Resources

Jesus Revival: Returning To Our First Love
©Jay Morgan 2022

All rights reserved. No part of this publication may be reproduced, distributed, or transmitted in any form or by any means, including photocopying, recording, or other electronic or mechanical methods, without the prior written permission of the publisher, except in the case of brief quotations embodied in critical reviews and certain other noncommercial uses permitted by copyright law. For permission requests, write to the publisher, addressed "Attention: Permissions Coordinator," at the address below.

The author's intent is to offer information of a spiritual nature that will educate the reader in the search for spiritual well-being. The author nor publisher shall have neither liability nor responsibility to any person or entity with respect to any loss or damage caused, or alleged to have been caused, directly or indirectly, by the information contained in this book.

Although the author and publisher have made every effort to ensure that the information in this book was correct at press time, the author and publisher do not assume and hereby disclaim any liability to any party for any loss, damage or disruption caused by errors or omissions, whether such errors or omissions result from negligence, accident, or any other cause.

All scripture quotations, unless otherwise indicated, are taken from the Holy Bible, New International Version®, NIV®. Copyright ©1973, 1978, 1984, 2011 by Biblica, Inc.TM Used by permission of Zondervan. All rights reserved world-wide. www.zondervan.com The "NIV" and "New International Version" are trademarks registered in the United States Patent and Trademark Office by Biblica, Inc.TM

Scripture quotations marked (NASB) are taken from the New American Standard Bible® Copyright © 1960, 1962, 1963, 1968, 1971, 1972, 1973, 1975, 1977, 1995 by The Lockman Foundation Used by permission. www.Lockman.org

Scripture quotations marked (NLT) are taken from the Holy Bible, New Living Translation, copyright ©1996, 2004, 2015 by Tyndale House Foundation. Used by permission of Tyndale House Publishers, Inc., Carol Stream, Illinois 60188. All rights reserved.

Scripture quotations marked (ESV) are from the Holy Bible, English Standard Version®, copyright © 2001 by Crossway, a publishing ministry of Good News Publishers. Used by permission. All rights reserved.

Scripture quotations marked (MSG) are taken from THE MESSAGE, copyright © 1993, 2002, 2018 by Eugene H. Peterson. Used by permission of NavPress. All rights reserved. Represented by Tyndale House Publishers, Inc.

Book Cover and Design: Jason Morgan
Editors: Kristin Spann, Wendy Smith, Angie Steffey

ISBN 979-8-9856015-6-5

Printed in the United States of America

Published by: APC Resources
APC Resources is the publishing division of the Appalachia Prayer Center/APC Ministries.
www.apcwv.com

*To the Church—the Bride of Jesus.
May we awake and return to our first love.*

Contents

SECTION I: REVIVAL 5

1. What is Revival? 6
2. A Jesus Revival 12
3. The Conditions of Revival 21

SECTION II: IT'S ALL ABOUT JESUS 35

4. Jesus-Centered Gospel 36
5. Jesus-Centered Lives 57
6. Jesus-Centered Accountability 69
7. Jesus-Centered Gatherings 80
8. Jesus-Centered Preaching 88
9. Jesus-Centered Outreach 99
10. Jesus-Centered Ministry 107
11. Jesus-Centered Leadership 118
12. Jesus-Centered Alliances 128

SECTION III: THE WAY FORWARD 141

13. Church as Usual Is Over 142

14. Subtle Dangers in the Contemporary Church 150

15. The Fire of a Revived Church 163

16. Preparing for the Future 178

APPENDICES 191

Appendix 1: Integrating Prayer into the Life of the Church 192

Appendix 2: A Healthy Discipleship Plan 194

SECTION I
REVIVAL

Chapter One
What is Revival?

In different yet consistent ways, the message of revival is resounding through the Church today. Many speak of America's "Third Great Awakening." Others see a worldwide harvest of millions of souls. Others are preaching a revival lifestyle that can and should be lived by all Christians. While revival is a buzzword in the church culture, few realize what it is and the implications that it brings. Let's begin by examining true revival.

When we think of revival movements, we typically think of spiritual fervor sweeping through a region and many people getting saved. Patrick Morley gives the following definition:

> *During revival, God supernaturally transforms believers and nonbelievers in a church, locale, region, nation, or the world through sudden, intense enthusiasm for Christ.*[1]

> *People sense the presence of God powerfully; conviction, despair, remorse, repentance, and prayer come easily; people thirst for God's word; many authentic conversions occur; and backsliders are renewed.* [2]

At the risk of mincing words, I will make the case that the lost turning to Jesus is not in and of itself revival. Rather, these moments of an observable move of God's presence in a community and its harvest are the *product* of revival.

The word revive means *to bring back to life or consciousness*.[3] One must have first been alive or awake to be brought *back* to consciousness. Therefore, it is the Church that needs to experience revival. My prayer is that the bride of Christ, the Church—once awake with love for Jesus but now lulled into spiritual complacency and slumber—would return to the fire and fervency of her first love for Christ. This is a *Jesus Revival*.

A renewed awakening of love for Jesus in His Church.

Have no doubt, when the Church is awakened and brought back to consciousness, the aforedescribed harvest follows. The intimacy between Christ and His bride results in the birth of many sons and daughters into the family of God.

Duncan Campbell, a leader in the great revival of the Hebrides Islands of Scotland in the 1940s-1950s, distinguishes revival from regular evangelism:

> *Revival is a community saturated with God. That is the difference between revival and successful evangelism.*

> *In successful evangelism, in successful crusades, you have ten, you have twenty saved here, you have a hundred brought to Christ there, but the community remains unchanged. Men move on to their Christless hell.*
>
> *But when God steps down, when hearts are made clean by Him, then He finds an avenue through which He can move; the community becomes saturated with God, so that many of those who find the Saviour come into saving relationship with Him before they come near any Church or place of meeting.[4]*

Revival is when a "community becomes saturated with God." What an incredible thought! But what produced such revival? A remnant of believers—two elderly sisters, one blind and the other crippled, later joined by a group of seven men who refused to give heaven no rest until God turned His face toward their island. These were people who experienced personal revival that overflowed into a saturation of the entire island by the Holy Spirit.

Duncan continues:

> *You have heard of the movement in the Hebrides; you have heard of the movement in the Congo; you have heard of the movement in Korea, in Brazil.*
>
> *Then you exclaim: "God can you do it again?" I want to say this, and I say it on the authority of this Book, yes, God will do it again when He*

finds a church He can trust; when He finds a man whom He can trust with revival.[5]

IS REVIVAL NECESSARY?

Many people criticize prayer for revival. Some would say that it is a shortcut to the hard work of reaching others through our personal witness. Others insist that the characteristics of revival should be seen in the lives of everyday Christians—that revival is a lifestyle to be lived out, not an event to be prayed for.

I agree. This is how an alive church should function. Christians should live in and demonstrate the power and presence of Christ in their lives.

But the problem is the state of the church.

When a body has lost its vitality and is dying, when the heart is not beating, when the spirit of breath has stopped, resuscitation efforts are necessary. Defibrillation paddles are laid to the chest, and a jolt of electricity is applied to bring the body back to life.

This is what revival is.

Jonathan Edwards, revivalist of the Great Awakening, described revival as "an acceleration and an intensification of the Holy Spirit's normal work."[6]

Acceleration and intensification. Shocking the church back to life and jolting the church back to consciousness and vitality. This is a revival season.

When you see the world around us and the decay of power in the church, the psalmist's desperate plea of, "Oh, that you would revive us again!"[7] should be commonplace in the church.

The tendency of the church after experiencing a season of revival is to return to spiritual slumber, or death, and wait for the next revival season. We must learn to live as a revived body (more about this later). But the current critical state of the church necessitates an accelerated and intensified saturation of the Holy Spirit's power in our communities.

Prayer for revival in the Church. We must begin praying for an awakening in the 200-million-plus professed American believers. If even half of them become spiritually vibrant, living in the power and presence of Christ, a great harvest will follow. So why is this urgent need for revival not commonly seen or sensed in the church?

Many do not see the church as asleep. If you are sleeping, you don't realize it until you wake up.

Some would point to their growing church numbers and baptisms as proof that their church is spiritually healthy. But are new believers showing evidence of new birth? Are the desires of Christ evident in them? Are they maturing into fervent, passionate evangelists?

Many point to their personal salvation as proof that they are spiritually vibrant. Are you bearing fruit in your life? Are you seeing the power of the Holy Spirit manifesting through you to impact the culture you live in?

While a lot of good is coming from many local churches, a look at the culture around us indicates that the Church, for the most part, is not the prevailing force that Jesus described, particularly when many professed Christians in American society seem to have completely lost their moral compass.

Just a small probe below the surface shows that too many have similar values and practices to the culture around them. The moment anyone points this out, they are quickly reprimanded for being "judgmental."

We must recognize we have a problem.

The church needs a spiritual awakening. Many who profess salvation are not actually saved, and many who are truly saved have been lulled into a false sense of security and see no reason to engage the culture around them.

Revival is not an option; it is the only lasting solution. When I see the state of the world, the decay of morality and loss of power in the church, the only response is to desperately plead, "Oh God, you must revive your sleeping church!"

> *Will you not revive us again, that your people may rejoice in you? Psalms 85:6*

Chapter Two
A Jesus Revival

The revival call we herald is for the bride of Jesus to return to "life or consciousness." In other words, to revive her passionate love for Jesus. When this happens, Jesus will be supreme in His Church's heart, motives, and adoration.

> *He is the head of the body, the church; he is the beginning and the firstborn from among the dead, so that in everything he might have the supremacy. Colossians 1:18*

THE SUPREMACY AND CENTRALITY OF CHRIST

Sadly, but probably not intentionally, it seems as if the bride of Jesus has made church about everyone and everything except our glorious Lord and Savior. We've made it about…

> Preachers and leaders.
> The congregation.
> The sermon series and delivery styles.

Music and worship leaders.
The date and styles of songs we sing.
The aesthetics of the room we gather to worship in.
The gifts of the Spirit—whether for or against.
Young vs. old.
Members vs. visitors.
The needs of the saved vs. the needs of the lost
and the list goes on . . .

Notice the following encouragement and desire expressed by the Apostle Paul to the Ephesian church:

> *For this reason, ever since I heard about your faith in the Lord Jesus and your love for all God's people, I have not stopped giving thanks for you, remembering you in my prayers. I keep asking that the God of our Lord Jesus Christ, the glorious Father, may give you the Spirit of wisdom and revelation, so that you may know him better. Ephesians 1:15-17*

Paul's prayer for the church at Ephesus was that a spirit of wisdom would come into the church, that people would receive greater revelation of Jesus.

Notice that he commended them in their faith. The faith of the first church was uniquely powerful. They did not have the momentum of two thousand years and billions of fellow believers. Yet they believed. Even so, Paul's prayer was that they would "know him better."

Maybe there's something that many are missing. Maybe there's more to Jesus than a salvation prayer. Maybe, just maybe, there is an untapped, infinite treasure to discover in Him.

Jesus is what we need.

We often desire healing, deliverance, rescue, fire. But Jesus is the healer, the deliverer, the Savior, and the one who burns with fire.

Jesus is what we need.

Maybe He is not part of God's plan—He is the plan. Maybe Jesus is not the means to the end, but is both the means and the end. He is the Treasure in the Field; He is the Pearl of Great Price.[8]

Jesus is what we need.

While many are attempting to find new revelation in Scripture and explore new depths of human understanding, maybe a fresh revelation of the ancient understanding of Jesus is needed.

Authors Viola and Sweet write:

> *Christians have made the Gospel about so many things—things other than Christ. But Jesus Christ is the gravitational pull that pulls everything together and gives it meaning. Without Him, all things lose their value. They are*

> *but detached pieces floating around in space. That includes your life.*
>
> *It is all too possible to emphasize a spiritual truth, value, virtue, or gift, yet miss Christ, who is Himself the embodiment and incarnation of all these things.*
>
> *Seek Christ, embrace Christ, know Christ, and you will have touched Him who is life. And in Him resides all truth, values, virtues, and gifts, in living color.* [9]

I have been involved in church leadership nearly all my life. I found it easy to get people excited about a service, a song, a minister, a message, a cause, an experience, a production, or even about "making a difference." But sadly, I have also found that few people—thankfully, they do exist—get excited about the pure presence of the Lord, stripped down with no additions. Just Jesus, face-to-face.

Those things have their place, but if any of them becomes more intriguing to our church than the real presence of Jesus, idolatry has crept in. And it must be identified, confessed, and repented of—turned away from. We must pray and fast until His presence fills our lives and gatherings, because once people truly behold Him, everything else becomes very trivial.

When God first began to challenge my church with this understanding, we were in a season of revival. It was one of the most unique demonstrations of God's presence and power that I had personally experienced up to that time, and maybe since.

During this time, we didn't announce singers and preachers. Even though people spoke, ministered, and led worship, it just wasn't about any of us. We simply invited people to come and experience Jesus. And the Jesus encounters were numerous and unexplainable. Like on the Day of Pentecost in Scripture, the aftereffects left us both amazed and perplexed. "Some mocked while others marveled."[10]

Among other things, we found that Jesus is the ultimate Revivalist. If you invite people into His presence, He will communicate to them and reach them in ways that normal teaching and worship events cannot. While those avenues are important, they are nothing compared to the way people personally encounter the Son of God when in His presence. Even people of other religions who did not believe that Jesus was the Son of God wept—against their control—in the presence of Jesus as they encountered Him.

This is why we cry out for revival. We cry out for God to release a prevenient grace on His Church so they will stir from their sleep, experience His power and presence, and passionately pursue Jesus to follow Him with their lives.

The best of sermons, sermon series, sets, lights, visual aids, or anything else we offer can only create interest in people. And this alone is not enough. People can become very interested in your church, preaching, and worship style, your mission and your vision, and still not know Christ.

People must become hungry for Jesus. Only true spiritual rebirth creates authentic spiritual hunger. Just as a baby needs, craves, and demands nourishment, so a born-again spirit will desire the Word and presence of Jesus.

True revival will focus on a return to the exaltation of Christ; He will return to His most supreme place in the Church, and He will draw all men to Himself. This is a *Jesus* revival.

WHY THE EMPHASIS ON JESUS?

Jesus is the foundational rock that the church—indeed everything—is built upon. All things were made by Jesus, for Jesus. He holds all things together.

> *For in him all things were created: things in heaven and on earth, visible and invisible, whether thrones or powers or rulers or authorities; all things have been created through him and for him. He is before all things, and in him all things hold together. Colossians 1: 16 -17*

The Father only spoke twice in the New Testament. Both times were to affirm the validity of Jesus.

> *And a voice from heaven said, "This is my Son, whom I love; with him I am well pleased." Matthew 3:17*

> *While he was still speaking, a bright cloud covered them, and a voice from the cloud said,*

> *"This is my Son, whom I love; with him I am well pleased. Listen to him!" Matthew 17:5*

The Father affirmed Jesus as Lord over all and Savior of the world.

> *Therefore let all Israel be assured of this: God has made this Jesus, whom you crucified, both Lord and Messiah. Acts 2:36*

Jesus is the way to the Father. To seek after God through any other avenue—spiritual or secular—is incomplete and will not lead to the Father. We are then stuck, often even as professed Christians, living a purposeless, hopeless, joyless life, because we are not finding and doing the will of the Father as revealed though Jesus. *He* is the way.

> *Jesus answered, "I am the way and the truth and the life. No one comes to the Father except through me." John 14:6*

Jesus reveals the glory of the Father.

> *For God, who said, "Let there be light in the darkness," has made this light shine in our hearts so we could know the glory of God that is seen in the face of Jesus Christ. 2 Corinthians 4:6 NLT*

Jesus' life and teachings show us the will of the Father.

> *Anyone who does not love me will not obey my teaching. These words you hear are not my own; they belong to the Father who sent me. John 14:24*

Jesus' death and resurrection give us the power to do the will of the Father.

> *For we died and were buried with Christ by baptism. And just as Christ was raised from the dead by the glorious power of the Father, now we also may live new lives. Romans 6:4 NLT*

Faith in Jesus brings us back to spiritual life so we can live as sons and daughters of the Father.

> *If you declare with your mouth, "Jesus is Lord," and believe in your heart that God raised him from the dead, you will be saved. Romans 10:9*

> *But as many as received him, to them gave he power to become the sons of God, even to them that believe on his name: John 1:12 KJV*

Jesus is the way to the Holy Spirit. When people wonder why revival has not come to their church or community, the answer may be because their focus was not *first and foremost* on Jesus. Only He can baptize us with the Holy Spirit, and only the Holy Spirit can revive a dying church and world.

> *I baptize you with water for repentance. But after me comes one who is more powerful than I, whose sandals I am not worthy to carry. He will baptize you with the Holy Spirit and fire.*
> *Matthew 3:11*

The Holy Spirit reminds us of what Jesus taught and gives us the power to tell others about Him.

> *But the Helper, the Holy Spirit, whom the Father will send in my name, he will teach you all things and bring to your remembrance all that I have said to you. John 14:26 ESV*

> *But you will receive power when the Holy Spirit has come upon you, and you will be my witnesses in Jerusalem and in all Judea and Samaria, and to the end of the earth.*
> *Acts 1:8 ESV*

So, to say, "It's all about Jesus" is not an overstatement for a believer. It is the hinge-pin reality that we must rediscover.

Above all, this book is an effort to cry out—in a John the Baptist, forerunner manner—the Lord is coming! Be prepared! And when He does come, we will forever say, "Behold, the Lamb of God, who takes away the sins of the world!" (John 1:29).

May the church, the purchased bride of Christ, be once again enthralled by her bridegroom Jesus.

Chapter Three
The Conditions of Revival

Those who long for revival must confront the frustrating reality that they cannot produce it through their own efforts. Revival is a sovereign move of God in a community. The effects of it are so abnormal and profound, only God could orchestrate it. Churches cannot "drum up" or "hype up" revival. Many try and fail.

But here's the good news: While we cannot force God to send revival, we can certainly do things that attract His presence.

> *For the eyes of the Lord are toward the righteous, and his ears attend to their prayer, but the face of the Lord is against those who do evil. 1 Peter 3:12 NASB*

> *On your walls, O Jerusalem, I have appointed watchmen; All day and all night they will never keep silent. You who remind the LORD take no rest for yourselves; And give Him no rest until He establishes and makes Jerusalem a praise in the earth. Isaiah 62:6-7 NASB*
>
> *You will seek Me and find Me when you search for Me with all your heart. Jeremiah 29:13 NASB*

God has a history of showing up where He is wanted! Revivalist Daniel Norris writes:

> *Revival always comes as a response. It is heaven's answer to the sustained cries and petitions of God's people who have firmly made up their minds that a move of God is the only solution.* [11]

Nearly every great awakening throughout Christian history was marked by a radical call to prayer, as well as repentance and consecration among Christians. It's interesting to note that these are predominantly foreign to the modern American/Western church. Not only that, but a great majority of Christians are outright offended if called toward either. But notice the clear directives the Lord gave in Scripture that would motivate Him to hear and respond to prayer:

> *If my people, who are called by my name, will humble themselves and pray and seek my face and turn from their wicked ways, then I will*

> *hear from heaven, and I will forgive their sin and will heal their land. 2 Chronicles 7:14*

These statements, to "pray and seek His face" and "turn from your wicked ways," are a call to prayer and consecration. This will wake the church from her slumber and create a holy, fervent fire of desire for the bridegroom Jesus. He will answer that desire with His presence.

And while we wait for His coming, let us refuse to settle for anything less than Him. Like the heartbroken lover in the Song of Songs, may we search for our Beloved. Notice the way that Eugene Peterson paraphrases the young woman's passionate pursuit:

> *Restless in bed and sleepless through the night, I longed for my lover. I wanted him desperately. His absence was painful. So I got up, went out and roved the city, hunting through streets and down alleys. I wanted my lover in the worst way! And then the night watchmen found me . . . "Have you seen my dear lost love?" I asked. No sooner had I left them than I found him . . . I threw my arms around him and held him tight, wouldn't let him go until I had him home again. Song of Songs 3:1–4 MSG*

Let us remain lovesick until He arrives with all of His love, power, and might.

REVIVAL IS NOT A CHURCH-GROWTH SHORTCUT

Be warned: The fire and spiritual fervency that results from prayer and consecration will quickly be rejected by many today. In most Christian circles, passion about your church, worship experiences, worship team, pastor, mission, cause, brand, or denomination is completely acceptable and encouraged. But the moment saints become spiritually fervent about prayer and the biblical call to consecration, many people get uncomfortable. And for good reason.

A return to prayer and consecration separates the wheat from the chaff. There are too many looking to the church and to God to solely fulfill their needs, while God, beginning with Adam, has been searching for those who will give themselves fully to His cause. This total abandonment to Christ only comes through the Holy Spirit's purifying fire and presence.

Satan will tolerate and even encourage all sorts of passionate spiritual activity, but he earnestly resists prayer-fueled spiritual fervency in church. And rightfully so. Prayer and consecration revive—bring life and power—back to the church, resulting in his kingdom's demise.

Revival is initially very costly. It will most likely result in the pruning of the church to get it healthy. In a sleeping church, many unhealthy, sinful practices and people become commonplace. In its awakened state, the Holy Spirit will call for change, and if people refuse to listen to His convicting voice, He will prune them from His body.

> *Every branch in Me that does not bear fruit, He takes away; and every branch that bears fruit,*

> *He prunes so that it may bear more fruit. John 15:2 NASB*

Revivalist and author John Burton writes:

> *Revival isn't marked by a full house. Revival starts in a room that reveals the remnant. The revival that erupted in that roomful of remnants [on Pentecost] resulted in explosive church growth and kingdom advance.*
>
> *Premature church growth will result in a multiplication of lukewarm, dead and dying people who have no idea what it feels like to have tongues of fire igniting over top of them.* [12]

A RETURN TO PRAYER

All of the mighty people of God in Scripture were people of prayer. Enoch walked with God. Moses desired God's glory more than anything else. The prophets were given revelation in prayer. Jesus often withdrew and prayed.

Every great move of God in history was prefaced by seasons of intense prayer. Pentecost, the Celtic Church Movement, the Moravian Mission Movement, the life and ministry of John Wesley, the Fulton Street Prayer Revival, the Welsh Revival, and the Hebrides Island Revival are all examples of God pouring out His Spirit on people of prayer.

Duncan Campbell recounts the power of the Hebrides Island Revival in 1949:

> *A number of men and two elderly women there were made conscious of the desperate need of their parish; all human effort had failed and had left them baffled. They realized that their one resource was to fall back upon God.*
>
> *Oh, how true it is that despair often is the womb from which real faith is born. When man comes to the end of himself . . . he has reached the beginning of God.*[13]

The Great Revival that swept Wales in 1904–1905 was not only birthed in prayer but was indeed a prayer revival. Describing it, James E. Stewart wrote:

> *It was praying that rent the heavens; praying that received direct answers there and then. The Spirit of intercession was so mightily poured out that the whole congregation would take part simultaneously for hours!*
>
> *Strangers were startled to hear the young and unlettered pray with such unction and intelligence as they were swept up to the Throne of Grace by the Spirit of God.*
>
> *Worship and adoration were unbounded. Praise began to mingle with the petitions as answered prayer was demonstrated before their very eyes. Often when unsaved loved ones were the focus of the intercession, they would*

be compelled to come to the very meeting and be saved![14]

Satan will fight the call for fervent prayer and consecration because it is there that God exposes and burns away sin, and we become pure; we become victorious. It is in prayer and consecration that we begin to see the heart of the Father, to understand His vision in the world as well as His desire from us. We begin to learn about His Kingdom and get our marching orders. Our own agenda is brought into alignment with the Father's, and we begin to pray even as Jesus did, "Not my will but Your will be done."[15]

It is in passionate, settled, tarrying prayer and consecration that we receive Holy Spirit power, even as the disciples did on the day of Pentecost. The command was for them to *kathizo* (tarry)—literally settle in[16]—and wait for power. It came, and God added to their number daily those who were being saved (Acts 2:47). This is revival. Not all prayer is private. Scripture and church history are full of examples of the power that is only accessed through praying with others.

Jesus' Example. Jesus stated that two or three gathered in His name bring power.[17]

The early Church's example. The early Church gathered and tarried in prayer until they received power.[18] The same met together and prayed for the Apostle Peter after he was put in prison. While they prayed, God sent an angel to release him.[19] Paul and Silas prayed together in prison, and God released earth-shaking power that came and set them free.[20]

Jesus Revival

Moravian Missions movement. In the 1700s, Moravian Christians lived on communal property due to outside persecution. Division crept in. Then, corporate prayer was called. According to their account, the Holy Spirit was poured out on the entire assembly.

What ensued was a 100-year, 24-hour-a-day prayer meeting; subsequently, hundreds from that first group gave their lives to serve in world missions. Some historians credit this movement with spurring the First Great Awakening in the United States. It was during this time, through the influence of the Moravians, that John Wesley encountered the Holy Spirit and became a great revivalist.[21]

Fulton Street Prayer Revival. In 1857, God moved upon Reverend Jeremiah Lanphier to gather people at noon to pray on Fulton Street in New York. Within eighteen months, similar prayer groups had formed in cities all over the U.S. An estimated one million people gave their lives to Jesus—all through corporate prayer meetings.[22]

Cane Ridge Revival. From August 6–12, 1801, believers from Cane Ridge, Kentucky, who attended different churches met together for prayer and communion, an annual three-to-five day meeting that ended with the Lord's Supper. Typically, people gathered in the dozens, maybe the hundreds. However, at this Cane Ridge Communion, as many as 20,000 people arrived.

What ensued was a revival that brought salvation to thousands of people. Vanderbilt historian Paul Conkin said that it was "arguably . . . the most important religious gathering in all of American history."[23]

The Welsh Revival. Prayer gripped young Welshman Evan Roberts and his spiritual companions in 1904. He attended a prayer meeting and asked those who were seeking a deeper spiritual life to stay behind. Together they prayed and gave themselves to the cause of Christ; as a result, revival hit the entire island of Wales. Tens of thousands were saved.

The revival was a leading story in major newspapers. Lists of people who converted were even printed in local town newspapers. Popular, national sporting events were cancelled or postponed due to the impact of the revival on the nation. Bars and gambling establishments were shut down. Factories temporarily closed for daytime prayers, as public prayer meetings became a major vehicle for revival. [24]

The Hebrides Island Revival. In the Hebrides islands of Scotland, people set their hearts to pray, and God sent revival. Thousands were born again into the Kingdom of God between 1949 and 1952.[25]

Should you have a personal relationship with God? Absolutely. Should you pray individually? Absolutely. Jesus gave us that example. But He also commanded and desired His disciples to pray together with Him.[26]

Those who resist and make no time for corporate prayer do not do so at the prompting of the Holy Spirit. There are typically other factors at play, such as an overcrowded agenda or priorities not ordered by God's Word. The cares of this world are choking the very spiritual life out of Jesus' Church.

A RETURN TO CONSECRATION

The great revivalist of America's Second Great Awakening, Charles Finney, stated:

> *Revival is a renewed conviction of sin and repentance, followed by an intense desire to live in obedience of God. It is giving up one's will to God in deep humility.*[27]

This is a return to consecration—conviction of sin and a desire to live in obedience to Christ. Duncan Campbell recounts how a desire for holiness gripped the praying remnant on the Hebrides Isle of Lewis:

> *So they waited and the months passed and nothing happened; until one morning a young man in the company read the portion of Psalm 24 . . . "Who shall ascend into the hill of the Lord, or who shall stand in His holy place? He that hath clean hands and a pure heart" . . . He shall receive the blessing of the Lord."*

> *...And then he prayed, "Are my hands clean, is my heart pure?"*

> *He got no further. At that moment there came to them a realization of God, an awareness of His presence that lifted them from the sphere of the ordinary into the sphere of the extraordinary...Revival had come and the power that was let loose in that barn shook the whole community of Lewis.*

These few men—and two elderly women—discovered this profound truth, that a God-sent revival must ever be related to holiness, and real New Testament separation. . . . revival was coming, God was going to be honored, they were going to see men so supernaturally altered that holiness would characterize every part of their being, body, soul and spirit. That was the truth that gripped them.[28]

Prayer is *being* with Jesus. Consecration—conviction of sin and a desire to live in obedience to Him—is the *result* of being with Jesus.

> *And I will give you a new heart, and I will put a new spirit in you. I will take out your stony, stubborn heart and give you a tender, responsive heart. And I will put my Spirit in you so that you will follow my decrees and be careful to obey my regulations.*
> *Ezekiel 36:26-27 NLT*

God said, "I will put my Spirit in you so that you will follow . . . and obey." Spiritual rebirth empowers people to follow God's commands. It is not a "license" or excuse to be exempt from them.

Perhaps you've seen something similar to the following:

> *Jacob was a cheater. Peter had a temper. Paul was a murderer. Thomas was a doubter. Mary was a prostitute. But God used them.*

This is true. However, each one of these people repented of their ways and turned to God. They did not stay the same. They were transformed by God.

We must preach repentance from sin and surrender to the Lordship of Jesus to the lost, unbelieving world. But to those who are saved, we must preach consecration—living a life surrendered to Jesus, which means *continued* turning from sin and following Jesus in one's everyday life. If Jesus is Lord, it will impact the way we live.

Many people want to:

> Be a Christian without being changed.
> Be pardoned for their crimes but remain a criminal.
> Be assured of their salvation and continue to sin.
> Believe they are saved without being sanctified.
> Believe they are right without becoming righteous.
> Go to heaven without becoming holy.

Some would teach salvation without surrender to Christ. They preach Christ as Savior, but not Christ as Lord. Obedience to Christ is falsely viewed as optional or something only some Christians attain to. Too often, the concept of forgiveness of sin is *overemphasized*, and the concept of repentance—turning from sin and being spiritually reborn—is *underemphasized*.

When the angel announced Jesus' birth to Mary, he said that Jesus would "save His people from their sins." [29] It is important to understand that we are saved *from* our sins, not just forgiven the penalty of our sins. We must repent—or turn from—our way of doing things and make Jesus the Lord of our life, fully trusting in Him. This means following Him as Lord, not just saying that He is Lord.

If a person truly believes in their heart and surrenders their will to Jesus' Lordship, they will be born again. The Holy Spirit will give them assurance of their rebirth, and then evidence of the new birth will be present. This evidence is the *new desires* of a spiritually reborn son or daughter of God.

Believers can still sin. We have patterns of sin engrained in our fleshly nature that we must overcome. However, if we do sin, we experience the discipline of the Lord; He will put us back on the right path and we will begin to develop a hatred of our sin. This does not involve hating other sinners, but rather an intense desire to have God free us from the sin that so easily binds *us*.

The question is not, *"Do I ever still have a desire to sin?"* It is, *"Are there new desires for righteousness present in me?"* And *"When I sin, do I experience the discipline of the Lord? Does He correct me? Is He placing a hatred for that sin in my heart?"*

Sadly, too many want the love of the Father without His discipline. But He corrects the child He loves (Hebrews 12:6). This means we can't do everything we want to do. Too many want the forgiveness of the Son without the new life He brings. But if He is your Lord, old things pass away, all things become new.[30]

Too many want the peace and power of the Holy Spirit without His purifying fire. We want comfort without conviction. But He is the one who comforts *and* convicts us of sin, righteousness, and judgment.[31]

Jesus Revival

Passionate love for Jesus is the only thing that will correct this thinking. This is why we cry out for a Jesus Revival to come to the church.

SECTION II
IT'S ALL ABOUT JESUS

Chapter Four
Jesus-Centered Gospel

A Jesus Revival will first and foremost cause a return to preaching a Jesus-centered Gospel. Old Testament prophets were appointed by God to call His people back to the tenets of their covenant with Him. In the same manner, He is raising up prophetic voices in this time, calling the church back to the tenets of the true covenant of grace and to *Who* Jesus is.

The church seems to have lost its way. A counterfeit gospel that does not emphasize the Lordship of Jesus in the everyday lives of His people, one that does not emphasize the need to repent from sin and follow Him, has crept into the Church. The deception is so subtle that it would deceive the very elect if possible.

> *For the time will come when they will not endure sound doctrine; but wanting to have their ears tickled, they will accumulate for themselves teachers in accordance to their*

> *own desires, and will turn away their ears from the truth and will turn aside to myths. 2 Timothy 4:3-4 NASB*

An alarming, growing number of professed Christians do not know what true, sound doctrine is. Some know the traditions of men, and others know the opinions of a secular world, but most know very little of what Jesus and the apostles taught.

Let's be clear. The true Gospel message, as preached by Jesus and the apostles, will emphasize the following:

> **The Lordship of Jesus.** Jesus is the only way that we can be spiritually reborn and returned to the Father.

> **Repentance from sin.** People must be called to turn away from sin and surrender to Jesus. Therefore, a biblical understanding of sin must be preached. One that conveys that the wages of sin is death and destruction in this life and ultimately eternal death, which is eternal separation from God in hell.

> **The cost of discipleship.** It's true that salvation is by grace through faith. However, the Christian life is one of holiness. We live as Jesus did through His power. By the power of the Holy Spirit, one must turn from their old life of sin and follow Jesus to new life.

PREACHING THE LORDSHIP OF JESUS

Preaching that salvation comes only through Jesus puts us at odds with the spirit of this age. People are considered intolerant or bigoted if they think that all religions are not equally valid. We are continually told to keep our faith private and to ourselves. The idea propagated is this: *While your faith might be right for you, it is rude and unloving to "force" your faith on other people.*

We are taught to live and let live. In some cultures of the world, it is illegal to share your religion with others, and doing so can result in punishment, imprisonment, or even death.

Jesus stated that He is the only way to God (John 14:6). If you believe Him, then religions that promote other ways present a false gospel. Following their teaching amounts to idolatry—false worship. A subtle—and sometimes not so subtle—message of "universalism" is filling the church. This teaching, in various forms, insists that all roads lead to heaven. That God is at work in all religions, drawing mankind to Himself.

This belief is most obvious when someone dies. Nearly everyone who dies is referred to as being in a "better place," dancing with the angels, or partying in heaven. But if Scripture is true, most people are *not* in a better place when they die.

> *Enter through the narrow gate; for the gate is wide and the way is broad that leads to destruction, and there are many who enter through it. For the gate is small and the way is narrow that leads to life, and there are few who find it. Matthew 7:13-14 NASB*

To be clear, the offer for salvation is open to everyone: "For whoever shall call on the name of the Lord shall be saved" (Romans 10:13 AKJV). To accept it, you must turn from your way to Jesus' way. Few are willing to do that.

> *He is the way.* He opened the way to the Father through His death and resurrection (Hebrews 4:14-16).
>
> *He is the truth.* If He is truth, then anything that contradicts what He said or how He lived is deceit (John 12:48).
>
> *He is the life.* We were dead in trespasses and sins, but God has made us alive through Christ Jesus (Ephesians 2:1-5).

What gives Jesus the right to be Lord, to have the final word in our lives? To answer this, we must understand Who He is.

- Jesus has eternally existed as the Word of God. He has always been with God, and He is God (John 1:1).
- Jesus became human, but He was also divine, or God (Colossians 1:15; John 1:14).
- While Jesus was on earth, God audibly spoke to the disciples and told them to listen to Him. In other words, He is Lord (Matthew 17:5).
- Jesus Himself claimed to speak for God (John 12:48-49).
- Jesus claimed to be the only way to God. This is true because He is God. It's illogical to think that you can get to God, aside from God (John 14:6).

- He earned the right to be Lord when He redeemed us—purchased us from sin and death through the sacrifice of His own body (1 Corinthians 6:19-20).
- Jesus validated who He said He was—God in the flesh sent to redeem humanity—through signs and wonders and ultimately through defeating death (Acts 2:22, 24, 36).

PREACHING REPENTANCE

To preach the full Gospel of Scripture, we must preach these things:

- We have all sinned and missed the mark (Romans 3:23).
- We are all guilty of violating God's law and are in serious trouble. Like sheep, we have all gone astray, after our own way (Isaiah 53:6).
- This means that people are not inherently good—morally or spiritually. We all have a sin nature that produces death in us (Romans 5:12).
- We are all separated from God because of our sin. We will spend eternity separated from Him unless we turn from our sin and surrender to Jesus (Matthew 25:41).

Peter preached Jesus as the Lord and Savior of all, for those who repent. The word *repent* means to "turn" or "change your mind."[32] He pleaded with them to turn away from their corrupt generation or culture, and directly linked this to being saved.

> *"Therefore let all Israel be assured of this: God has made this Jesus, whom you crucified, both Lord and Messiah." When the people heard this, they were cut to the heart and said . . . "Brothers, what shall we do?" Peter replied, "Repent and be baptized, every one of you, in the name of Jesus Christ for the forgiveness of your sins. And you will receive the gift of the Holy Spirit. With many other words he warned them; and he pleaded with them, "Save yourselves from this corrupt generation."*
> *Acts 2:36-38, 40*

The Apostle Paul reiterated that surrendering to Jesus' Lordship is necessary for salvation.

> *If you confess with your mouth Jesus as Lord, and believe in your heart that God raised Him from the dead, you will be saved.*
> *Romans 10:9 NASB*

Understand that true salvation is not a pass to get into heaven if you merely say a few "magic" words or articulate a right belief. Believing in God, and Jesus as the Son of God, is not enough to save you; even demons believe this.[33] Sensing the presence of God, performing miracles, saying a prayer, or being baptized also are not complete indications of salvation.

While these things are *important*, they are, at best, an acknowledgment or mental agreement with spiritual concepts, or a performing of spiritual activity. According to

Romans 10:9, this is not enough to save you. You must "believe *in your heart*" to be saved.

Since the heart is the center of the will, to truly believe in your heart that Christ is Lord involves a surrender of your life and will to His authority. It means you will live in obedience to His will and desires. Notice this question by Jesus: "Why do you call me, 'Lord, Lord,' and do not do what I say?" (Luke 6:46).

If Jesus is truly *your* Lord, obedience to His will is a normal response. Although self-sufficient people might acknowledge or agree with who Jesus is, they—along with Satan and his demons—will never submit to Jesus' Lordship. They will not trust Jesus enough to leave their sin and surrender their will and desires—the control of their life—to Him.

This inherently implies that we must explain what sin is and compel people to turn from it toward God's love, which will save them from both sin and its consequences. Many in the church do not know what biblical sin is or how to identify it. Some highlight trivial things or arbitrarily cherry-pick and debate what Levitical laws to enforce, with no real understanding of the Law or which parts were fulfilled through Christ. As a Christian, God's Word—not people's opinions, our culture, or our family's traditions—must determine our moral compass.

A good place to start is understanding the moral principles found throughout Scripture. This begins with the Ten Commandments, which Jesus expands in His teachings. They can also be seen in the apostles' teachings. (Refer to Matthew chapters 5-7, Galatians 5:19-21, Ephesians 5:3-5,

Colossians 3:5, 1 Corinthians 6:9-10, Revelation 21:8, and Romans 1:29-32.)

These passages outline Christ's basic teachings, as well as thoughts and behaviors called sinful works of the flesh. The warning is repeatedly clear that if we do not turn from these sins, we will not inherit the Kingdom of God.

Many in our contemporary culture—even multitudes within the church itself—have a dull conscience regarding sin, and they recoil at the thought of anyone telling them that their actions are wrong. "Judge not lest ye be judged" is spouted as an exemption from obeying any directive from Scripture. While our culture is not ready for this message, it desperately needs to hear it. Jesus came to set us free from the devil and destroy his work in the world.[34] Specifically, these are some sins listed in Scripture that God deeply desires to free us from:

> *Sexual promiscuity.* This includes heterosexual sex outside the bounds of marriage—"fooling around" with your boyfriend, girlfriend, or fiancé. It also includes homosexual sex and pornography—a form of lust. Obscene language, along with crude jokes, and other things that would devalue the gift of sexuality are also forbidden. Dressing or presenting oneself sensually to incite lust in others, leering at the opposite sex, and allowing lustful thoughts and actions to drive you is also sin.
>
> *Materialism (a form of idolatry).* The desire for more and more is rooted in greed and covetousness, and runs the risk of placing things,

even good things, over your relationship with God. Pursuing many facets of the American Dream puts us at high risk of idolatry.

Jealousy and envy in overcompetitiveness. So much of our society is driven to "keep up with" or do better than others. Often, people in the church and the world are driven by a typically unconscious desire for superiority. We obsess over sports, competition and winning. These behaviors can be deeply rooted in jealousy and envy.

Gossip, slander, and stirring up hatred between groups. According to Jesus, hatred in one's heart constitutes murder. Don't allow anger to drive you—both the church and the world are being swept up into polarizing, hate-filled vitriol over the ever-increasing political tensions of the day.

Pride and arrogance. This includes feeling superior and bullying people with words, ideas, and opinions, as well as spreading and consuming gossip and slander. It applies to social media as well as other communication.

Living non-sober. This encompasses using drugs and alcohol for intoxicating purposes, as well as wild partying and causing trouble, all in the name of "fun."

These sins, as well as others listed in Scripture, separate us from God. They make us live in bondage to the god of this world—Satan. We must call people out of sinful lifestyles and show them the way of salvation—turning from sin, submitting their lives fully to the Lordship of Jesus, and being baptized and led by the Holy Spirit so they will not fulfill the lusts of the flesh, but rather their God-designed purpose in life.[35]

Many will argue that it is not necessary to list sins specifically, for fear the sins may be misunderstood. Others insist that the Holy Spirit will teach believers what sin is, so there is no need for people to point to any specific action as wrong. Why, then, do we have Scripture? Why did the apostles write letters with lists of things for people to avoid? As we call people to turn from sin, we don't make new lists for them. We simply read Scripture and in love, warn them of what it says.

If a person does not realize they are sick, they will never seek treatment. In the same way, if a person does not know they are guilty of sin, they will never see their need for a Savior.[36]

This can produce a lot of issues in our culture and puts us in tension with the spirit of our age, which condemns any view as hateful and bigoted that disapproves of another's actions. While a person might have a legal right to do many things that Scripture calls sin, it does not mean they will not suffer the spiritual consequences of sin—death and hell. If we love people, we will humbly warn them of their spiritual condition and its consequences, even if we are scorned for doing so. If our Gospel is true, it is unloving to *not* tell people the truth.

Because of sin, people are separated from God and are spiritually restless. They often feel guilt and desire peace in their hearts. How will we offer them peace? Will we tell them of their condition and the solution—repent and surrender? Or will we convince them that they are okay and shouldn't feel guilty? That God's love means that they can stay just as they are, without any ill effect?

This makes about as much sense as taking the batteries out of a smoke alarm in a smoke-filled house. The discomfort of the alarm lets us know something is wrong. The great Christian writer C. S. Lewis wrote this:

> *Pain insists upon being attended to. God whispers to us in our pleasures, speaks in our consciences, but shouts in our pains. It is his megaphone to rouse a deaf world.*[37]

Lewis went on to explain that if God did not allow pain in our lives, we might never see our desperate need for Him.

Remember the real Gospel message: God created us to be His family. Then, He watched His creation, His children, leave Him and join His enemy. He knew they would suffer the same fate as Satan—eternal separation from Him in hell. He knew we could not save ourselves. So, through Jesus, He clothed Himself in flesh and came to rescue us.

This brings to mind a few key points:

God saved us because of His love, not because we are lovable.

> *But God demonstrates his own love for us in this: While we were still sinners, Christ died for us. Romans 5:8*

Scripture is clear: we had become God's enemies and were deserving of wrath. Yet, He made a way for our salvation.

> *Once you were alienated from God and were enemies in your minds because of your evil behavior. Colossians 1:21*
>
> *All of us also lived among them at one time, gratifying the cravings of our flesh and following its desires and thoughts. Like the rest, we were by nature deserving of wrath. Ephesians 2:3*

He did this because of His merciful lovingkindness—His grace.

> *For it is by grace you have been saved, through faith—and this is not from yourselves, it is the gift of God—not by works, so that no one can boast. Ephesians 2:8-9*

When we truly understand the horrific death Jesus went through for us, and that we did nothing to earn His love, we understand the honor that is due Him. We realize our need for salvation. Then and only then can we truly understand the gift we can receive through His sacrifice.

Even as the apostles before, we must plead with people to save themselves from this generation. Then we must preach that salvation comes only one way—through Jesus.

> *With many other words he warned them; and he pleaded with them, "Save yourselves from this corrupt generation."*
> Acts 2:40

If we are honest, it is usually not love for other people that keeps us from sharing the Gospel, it is fear. We fear rejection, or worse. The truth is, sharing the Gospel is not always comfortable or easy.

THE COST OF DISCIPLESHIP

Many preach that salvation is the way to an easier life. Following Jesus is viewed as a means to get what you want from God. Jesus did not preach this gospel. He warned His first disciples that the world would hate them; following Him would come at a cost.

> *If the world hates you, keep in mind that it hated me first. If you belonged to the world, it would love you as its own. As it is, you do not belong to the world, but I have chosen you out of the world. That is why the world hates you.*
> John 15:18-19

Jesus is the Way to the authentic, abundant life you are created to live. He is the Treasure of heaven. When you have Him, you have what you were made for. However, living for Jesus can often come with persecution. But when that happens, He told us to "Rejoice, for great is your reward in heaven!"[38]

Think of it like this: Imagine you board an airplane, and the crew gives you a parachute, saying that it will make your flight more enjoyable. After a few minutes of wearing the parachute, feeling its weight, and struggling with the inconvenience of it strapped to your back while sitting in a seat, you become frustrated and take it off. Obviously, the parachute is not making your flight more enjoyable.

Now imagine you board a plane, are handed a parachute, and given instructions to put it on. After a few minutes of flight you hear, "The plane is in trouble, and we're going to crash! Please use your parachute to jump to safety." Now your perspective has changed. The parachute is your lifeline. Even if it is temporarily inconvenient and cumbersome, it is no longer "burdensome," because it is your only chance to live.

At times, following Christ does not make life more enjoyable. It can feel inconvenient, cumbersome, and burdensome. But when you realize that imminent destruction is ahead and He is your only chance for salvation, His burden is no longer heavy.[39]

It is a joy to follow Him, no matter the temporary cost or inconvenience. When doing so brings pain or adversity, we must learn to live from the perspective of eternity, not from that of our immediate reality.[40] The Apostle Paul experienced a loss of everything that was important to him when he began following Jesus. His response?

> *I once thought these things were valuable, but now I consider them worthless because of what Christ has done. Yes, everything else is*

> *worthless when compared with the infinite value of knowing Christ Jesus my Lord. For his sake I have discarded everything else, counting it all as garbage, so that I could gain Christ. Philippians 3:7-8 NLT*

When you read Scripture, notice that Jesus never lowered the cost of discipleship, even if it meant that people would walk away from Him. Particularly interesting is the story of the rich young ruler who came to Jesus. Jesus asked him to sell all he had, give it to the poor, and follow Him. This was an obvious test of Jesus' Lordship in his life. Was he willing to leave all and follow Him? This request was not an indictment against owning personal property. Other disciples owned property. Jesus was testing to see if this man was willing to lay everything down for Him.

> *Jesus looked at him and loved him. "One thing you lack," he said. "Go, sell everything you have and give to the poor, and you will have treasure in heaven. Then come, follow me." At this the man's face fell. He went away sad, because he had great wealth. Mark 10:21-22*

Jesus loved this young man, but let him walk away. Jesus did not alter His message because of His love. And why should He? If His teachings lead to life, to change them would be preaching death.

It's interesting to note that while we might refer to the "cost of discipleship," what we gain far exceeds any cost, even if it costs everything. Like the man who sold all he owned to purchase a field that contained great treasure, what did he really lose?[41] Christian missionary Jim Elliot, who was killed at a young age while sharing the Gospel in Ecuador, wrote this:

> *He is no fool who gives what he cannot keep to gain what he cannot lose.*[42]

BE PREPARED FOR REJECTION

The true Gospel of Jesus will not always be met with acceptance. At times you will be rejected by the world and the church.

Rejection from the world. Paul received different responses when he shared the Good News of Christ:

> *At the phrase "raising him from the dead," the listeners split: Some laughed at him and walked off making jokes; others said, "Let's do this again. We want to hear more." But that was it for the day, and Paul left. There were still others, it turned out, who were convinced then and there, and stuck with Paul. Acts 17:32-34 MSG*

People will have different responses when hearing the Gospel. Some will reject it. Others will object to it because they need more information. And some will be ready to receive it.

Don't confuse objections with rejection. Some people are not necessarily rejecting Jesus; they have questions. These are usually rooted in control, fear, doubt, and/or shame. Be prepared to answer them.

> *But in your hearts revere Christ as Lord. Always be prepared to give an answer to everyone who asks you to give the reason for the hope that you have. But do this with gentleness and respect. 1 Peter 3:15*

On the other hand, we must "shake off" rejection.

> *Whatever town or village you enter, search there for some worthy person and stay at their house until you leave. As you enter the home, give it your greeting. If the home is deserving, let your peace rest on it; if it is not, let your peace return to you. If anyone will not welcome you or listen to your words, leave that home or town and shake the dust off your feet. Truly I tell you, it will be more bearable for Sodom and Gomorrah on the day of judgment than for that town. "I am sending you out like sheep among wolves. Therefore be as shrewd as snakes and as innocent as doves.*
> *Matthew 10:11-16*

This can be very difficult to do.

You might feel the need to beg or continue trying to convince someone to change and turn to Christ. Jesus never begged anyone to change. He wept over people who wouldn't change, but He didn't try to force them into a decision. Avoid pushing Christ onto others. Invest your time in people who are ready. Don't give up on those who aren't, but give them over to God and let Him continue to work in them. Keep praying for them, caring for them, and waiting for the right opportunity to help them come to Jesus.

Rejection from the "church." There will be a severe backlash against any Christian who stands for righteousness in the coming days. Don't be surprised if "Christians" will lead this persecution against the true Church of Jesus. Many in powerful Christian positions will succumb to the pressure of the world to promote tolerance of everyone and everything. They will distance themselves from all who are calling others to turn from sin toward righteousness and holiness, those standing for the truth that Jesus is the only way to heaven.

Those who call sin wrong will be condemned as unchristian, unloving, and judgmental—even by other "Christians." Those who claim that Christ is the only way to heaven will be told that they are narrow-minded, unloving, and not properly representing the true Gospel.

The truth is that many of the leaders of the church love power too much to give it up for the cause of Christ. So, they have created a tolerant, politically correct Christianity that *seems* like the Gospel, but in reality, is a perversion that will deceive the very elect, if possible.

Many in the church avoid the possibility of personal rejection by simply being silent. They will not actively call something sin when pushed. They will not preach against other religions as containing the "doctrines of devils." This is often rooted more in self-preservation than faithfulness to Jesus. The pressure, even by other Christians, is to "believe what you wish, but don't broadcast it everywhere." You will be told that "hate-filled" language is creating barriers keeping people from Jesus.

While many Christians are guilty of spewing hatred, disagreeing with someone's destructive decisions, warning them of the dangers of sin, and explaining salvation through Jesus is not hatred. It is love. By claiming that it's not Christlike to preach against sin or declare the Lordship of Jesus, many people are actually saying that quoting Jesus and His views will create a barrier that keeps people from Him. Jesus often encountered this backlash as well, but He was more interested in the condition of souls than how pleased people were with Him in the moment.

We must clearly understand that our battle is not with flesh and blood. No matter how upset people get when we warn them of the truth, we must not retaliate. We can speak in our defense as the Holy Spirit directs, but overcome evil with good through intensified prayer, greater fervency, and boldness in proclaiming the Gospel.

If we, as the church, become vicious and hateful toward others, we destroy our ability to free anyone from bondage. Is it wrong to speak the truth and ask people to turn from their sin toward Christ? No. Is it wrong to even plead and compel at appropriate times? No. Will we be accused of hate, even if we are not hateful? Often. Will our words be twisted to make us look like bigots and hate-mongers? Often.

But it is important that we keep a broken heart toward anyone who is still blinded by the god of this age. We must "be careful to live properly among [our] unbelieving neighbors. Then even if they accuse [us] of doing wrong, they will see [our] honorable behavior, and they will give honor to God when he judges the world." [43]

When threatened, do not be afraid. Instead, revere Christ as Lord. Be prepared to give an answer for what you believe. Be able to defend it, not just spout out clever one-liners and sound bites. And do so with gentleness and respect. Don't give people a reason to hate you. If they want to speak ill of you, they will have to make up lies or twist the truth.

> *But even if you suffer for doing what is right, God will reward you for it. So don't worry or be afraid of their threats. Instead, you must worship Christ as Lord of your life. And if someone asks about your hope as a believer, always be ready to explain it. But do this in a gentle and respectful way. Keep your conscience clear. Then if people speak against you, they will be ashamed when they see what a good life you live because you belong to Christ. Remember, it is better to suffer for doing good, if that is what God wants, than to suffer for doing wrong! 1 Peter 3:14-17 NLT*

We must see people who are bound in sin as victims of that sin. We must weep for their souls. Our hearts must break at the thought of their eternity without Christ. We cannot let fear of man stop our love for them. A love that cares enough to warn, no matter how they treat us in response.

And when you are persecuted, you must rejoice that God has counted you worthy to suffer disgrace for the name of Jesus.[44] If the world hated Jesus, it will hate us too!

> *If the world hates you, keep in mind that it hated me first. John 15:18*

Chapter Five
Jesus-Centered Lives

When we pray for Jesus to return to His supreme place in the church, we must first allow Him supremacy in our lives. As fully devoted followers, we must live lives that honor Him.

Christ is not just an idea or a person that lived and died two thousand years ago. He has eternally existed, and He is your creator and sustainer. All that you need in heaven and earth is found in discovering Him. Like the Apostle Paul, once we see the glory of God revealed in the face of Jesus, we will never again be the same. It changes our values, ambitions, goals, dreams, and actions (Phil. 3:7-8).

Let's review the Gospel message of Jesus:

Creation. God created the world as it should be. All things were created by Jesus, for Jesus. He desired to have a family to share for eternity. (Colossians 1:16).

The Westminster Catechism reminds us that mankind was created to "glorify God and enjoy Him forever."[45] We were given the mission to rule—bring the Kingdom of God to earth (Genesis 1:28). God gave the gift of human relationships in creating Eve for Adam, then gave them the shared job of ruling over the earth (Genesis 2:18).

Separation. Mankind separated themselves from a relationship with God by listening to the lies of Satan and pursuing their own desires (Genesis 3).

Each one of us was born into this separated state of sin (beginning with Adam and Eve). Each of us has gone our own way, departing from God (Romans 5:12, Isaiah 53:6, and Romans 3:23). Sin not only separates us from God, but it also brings death and destruction (Romans 6:23), where we share Satan's fate—hell (Matthew 25:41).

Redemption. God saw man in the fallen state he was in, and through Jesus, took on flesh and made a way for man to be reunited with Him (John 1 and Romans 5:8).

Jesus' life taught us the will of God—how to live as children of God (Hebrews 1:1-2). His death paid our death penalty (Romans 6:23; 1 John 2:2). His resurrection gives us the power to live a new life as a child of God (Romans 6:4-6).

Decision. Jesus did everything necessary to bring us to God, but He does not force us to trust and love God. We must each decide who we will follow. Will you live life your own way, or surrender to Jesus' Lordship in reconciliation with God (Romans 10:9-10)?

Salvation comes when we repent from our way and turn toward Jesus and follow His way. "For you were like sheep going astray, but now you have returned to the Shepherd and Overseer of your souls." (1 Peter 2:25).

- When we surrender to Jesus' Lordship, we are saved from our sins and are spiritually reborn (Romans 10:9-19; John 3:3).
- The Holy Spirit enters into us and gives us a new heart; He teaches us how to follow God's ways (Ezekiel 36:26-27).
- We then spend the rest of our lives living as Jesus' disciples—learning, obeying, and teaching others what He desires (Matthew 28:19-20).

The decision to surrender to the Lordship of Jesus is not just a decision about the afterlife. It has serious implications for your life now. Notice how Jesus made disciples when He walked the earth: "Leave all you know and follow me!" (Matthew 4:19-20). This is what it means to say that Jesus is Lord. If He is Lord, you obey Him. If you are Lord, you obey yourself (Luke 6:46). We must lose our old lives, become like a child, and relearn everything with Him in charge.

> *Whoever finds his life will lose it, and whoever loses his life for my sake will find it.*
> *Matthew 10:39 ESV*

> *Jesus answered him, "Truly, truly, I say to you, unless one is born again he cannot see the kingdom of God." John 3:3 ESV*

> *Truly, I say to you, unless you turn and become like children, you will never enter the kingdom of heaven. Matthew 18:3 ESV*

This involves leaving our desires to pursue Him and His will.

> *And he said to all, "If anyone would come after me, let him deny himself and take up his cross daily and follow me. Luke 9:23 ESV*

OBEDIENCE TO CHRIST

Jesus' life and teachings show us what new life is! Author David Platt writes:

> *It is impossible to be a follower of Christ while denying, disregarding, discrediting, and disbelieving the words of Christ.* [46]

How do we know the will of the Father? By listening to Christ.

> *For I did not speak on my own, but the Father who sent me commanded me to say all that I have spoken. John 12:49*

Jesus taught us that His words and teachings are spirit and life (John 6:63). This means that anything contrary to His teachings leads to death. If He says, "No," no matter how much you desire something, He is not being mean. He knows what is best.

If Christ is supreme in your life, His teachings will be supreme in your life as well. We cannot claim to love Him and yet live a lifestyle of disobedience.

> *Whoever says, "I know him," but does not do what he commands is a liar, and the truth is not in that person. But if anyone obeys his word, love for God is truly made complete in them. This is how we know we are in him: Whoever claims to live in him must live as Jesus did.*
> *1 John 2:4-6*

Remember, a Christian is not someone who simply believes in Jesus. A Christian is born again. Who you were is gone. You have been raised to new life. You live like Jesus through His power.

> *So all of us who have had that veil removed can see and reflect the glory of the Lord. And the Lord—who is the Spirit—makes us more and more like him as we are changed into his glorious image. 2 Corinthians 3:18 NLT*

Being "born again" is not a metaphor. A new spirit comes alive in us. We are no longer just sinners saved by grace.

> *This means that anyone who belongs to Christ has become a new person. The old life is gone; a new life has begun! 2 Corinthians 5:17 NLT*

> *I will give you a new heart and put a new spirit in you; I will remove from you your heart of stone and give you a heart of flesh. And I will put my Spirit in you and move you to follow my decrees and be careful to keep my laws.*
> Ezekiel 36:26-27

God saved us to conform us into Christ's image. This is true biblical holiness. We cannot have true Christianity without moving toward Christlikeness.

> *For those God foreknew he also predestined to be conformed to the image of his Son, that he might be the firstborn among many brothers and sisters.* Romans 8:29

UNDERSTANDING BIBLICAL DISCIPLESHIP

All of this becomes clearer once we understand the biblical meaning of the word *disciple*. Bill Hull notes that the New Testament understanding of it is one who *follows* or *emulates* Christ. [47]

The practice of making disciples is rooted in Hebrew rabbinic tradition, where students not only memorized their rabbi's words, but they also learned to *emulate* the rabbi's ministry, life, and character. Disciples in Jesus' day followed their rabbi wherever He went, learning from his teachings and training to act as he did.

> *In the world of the Bible, a disciple was a person who followed a teacher, rabbi, master, or*

> *philosopher. The disciple desired not only to learn the teaching of the rabbi, but to imitate the practical details of their life. A disciple did not merely attend lectures or read books, they were required to interact with and imitate a real living person. A disciple would literally follow someone in the hopes of eventually becoming what they are.*[48]

A student *learns* what their teacher *knows*, but a disciple *becomes* who their rabbi is. This is why the Apostle John wrote that one who says he abides in Jesus ought to walk in the same manner as Jesus walked.[49] In the book of Acts we learn that the first disciples of Jesus were called "followers of the Way."[50] They followed Jesus' way of life, based on His teachings.

This is not just a belief system. It is a way of living life that influences *every* decision that a disciple makes. This is why He commands us to teach new disciples to *obey* everything He commanded. He didn't just come to forgive us; He came to destroy evil's influence and teach us a new way to live.

> *The one who does what is sinful is of the devil, because the devil has been sinning from the beginning. The reason the Son of God appeared was to destroy the devil's work.* 1 John 3:8

We are not simply talking about attending worship services or memorizing some Bible verses and stories. Discipleship denotes actually becoming like Christ—in word and in deed!

Believing in God and believing that Jesus is the Son of God, the way to salvation, does not mean you are saved. As John Wesley taught in his great sermon, *Salvation by Faith*, this faith is no more than that of a demon.[51] No more than an intellectual agreement in spiritual concepts. In 2 Thessalonians 2:7-12, Paul teaches that those who reject the truth and believe that they can live in unrighteousness believe a lie and will be damned. This is strong language; it should be a sobering warning to the contemporary church.

Saving faith involves the surrender of your heart, will, and desires to Jesus. This is what it means to "believe in your heart" and surrender to His Lordship.[52] Jesus teaches that both wise and foolish people *listen* to Him, but only the wise obey Him. The foolish disobey Him. Professed salvation that is not followed by obedience to Christ clearly indicates a lack of real salvation.

To be clear, Christians are capable of sin and have besetting sins they must overcome. The question is, does the trajectory of an individual's life indicate obedience to Jesus? If not, this is a grave spiritual problem. You will not be perfect overnight, but are you allowing God to conform you into Jesus' image? If so, there will be evidence of a new nature in you.

True repentance and surrender produce a supernatural event. You are spiritually reborn. Your heart is regenerated by God. As often as needed, you can then be baptized and filled with the Holy Spirit. It gives you power. Strength. Endurance. Deliverance. Gifts. And much more.

True salvation produces a desire to be like Jesus.

Whoever claims to live in him must live as Jesus did.
1 John 2:6 NLT

Whoever says, "I know him," but does not do what he commands is a liar, and the truth is not in that person.
1 John 2:4

If you love me, keep my commands.
John 14:15

We must nurture the new desires that God places in us and let our roots grow deep. We must cooperate with the Holy Spirit and not grieve or quench His work in our lives. As we do these things, He conforms us into the image of Jesus.

LOVE-BASED OBEDIENCE

It comes down to answering these questions: *What means the most to me? Living a life focused on myself, which leads to sin and separation from God, or living a life that honors God because of my love for Him?*

Does love motivate your obedience to Christ?

Many Christians seem to see how much sin they can get away with, as if their attitude is, *"What is the least amount that I have to give up to be a Christian?"* Jesus' response is that the least amount is everything.

> *You cannot be my disciple, unless you love me more than you love your father and mother, your wife and children, and your brothers and*

> *sisters. You cannot come with me unless you love me more than you love your own life.*
> Luke 14:26 CEV

Surrendering to Jesus begins with giving Him your full allegiance and love. You will not *have the ability* to be His disciple if you do not love Him more than everything—including your own life.

In the verse above, Jesus points out that life demands a decision. Whatever you love most will be what you pursue. Christ calls you to live centered on loving God, loving others, and spreading His Kingdom. This runs opposite to the natural desire to live for yourself and worldly attachments. There will be conflict. You will have to make a choice. Your love and devotion to Jesus must be stronger than your worldly attachments and the sins that they produce.

Many of the first disciples and early Christians faced the severity of this choice. Many encountered betrayal by their own family and were killed for proclaiming their faith in Jesus. Throughout the centuries, Christians in various parts of the world have faced persecution, and it continues today. But they loved Jesus more than their comfort and physical safety. They loved Him more than anything this world has to offer.

This means that being a Christian involves more than going to church, trying to be a "good person," and avoiding a handful of taboo sins. The change goes much deeper than that. Your love for Him will alter your desires, ambitions, and motives. Your attachment to Him will become stronger than any other attachment in the world. You will desire to honor Him with all of your life.

You will discover security, worth, and fulfillment in Jesus. You will find meaning through your real identity as a child of God rather than through *substitute identities*. Love for Jesus—not obligation, guilt, or fear—will motivate your change.

This is why we must have a Jesus Revival in our personal lives first. We must burn with fire and love for our Bridegroom.

CONTINUED RESISTANCE TO CHRIST

Continued resistance to the Word of God and the work of the Holy Spirit means one of two things: either you have not truly been born again, and the Spirit of Christ does not live in you, or you are living in rebellion against God. Either way, it is a serious concern if you profess faith in Christ and willfully continue in patterns of sin without sorrow or repentance. Remember, there are many false assurances of salvation.

Did you truly give up control of your life to Jesus? Are you rebelling against His commands? Christians have the capacity to sin, but if they do, they will experience godly sorrow and His discipline, which puts them back on the right path. The ability to continue in sin without either indicates that you have never been saved.

Questions like these may seem judgmental. It is true that Jesus taught in Matthew 7:1-4 that we should not judge or condemn others—specifically, that we should not act like others' sins are worse than our own. However, in that same passage, He also taught that we should not believe the words of everyone who calls Him "Lord." Rather, we should examine the fruit their lives produce.

> *Beware of false prophets who come disguised as harmless sheep but are really vicious wolves. You can identify them by their fruit, that is, by the way they act . . . Yes, just as you can identify a tree by its fruit, so you can identify people by their actions.* Matthew 7:15-16, 20 NLT

Simply put, discipleship is being like Jesus. It is not simply learning what He taught, but to obey it. While the Christian life and faith are firmly centered on His teachings, obedience is possible only by relying on His Spirit as it fills a born-again heart. He conforms us to the image of Jesus.

Chapter Six
Jesus-Centered Accountability

If the Church truly centers around Jesus, then local churches will function as families of Jesus followers, as His body. People's pursuit of Christ and His likeness will become more important than their individual gifts or abilities. When we honor Jesus as the supreme head of the Church, His life will be the standard that we compare our lives to.

The public gatherings of churches often consist of guests, visitors, family, friends, onlookers, seekers, and skeptics. At some point, church leaders should be able to identify those with genuine faith in Jesus who desire to grow as His disciples. These constitute the fellowship of believers—members of the local body of Christ.

Pastors should responsibly oversee whether leaders and members of the local fellowship are indeed exhibiting Christlikeness. Scripture is clear that Christian leaders will give an account to God for those they care for. This is a tremendous responsibility. We cannot force others to do the right thing—manipulating and controlling them—but we must take care to cultivate the true character of Christ in our fellowships.

> *Have confidence in your leaders and submit to their authority, because they keep watch over you as those who must give an account. Do this so that their work will be a joy, not a burden, for that would be of no benefit to you.*
> Hebrews 13:17

Church leaders have a duty to *equip* people. The Holy Spirit will *empower* people. But we must also *expect* those who confess faith to live as disciples of Jesus.

If discipleship is emulating Christ, then Christlikeness will be evident in the lives of individual believers and the practices of congregations. The truth is, a great number of professed Christians do not have evidence of Christ in their lives. Tragically, they are often allowed to continue unchecked in their false beliefs. Revivalist and author Michael Brown writes:

> *You see, it's one thing to welcome the worst of sinners into our midst, showing them the love of God, introducing them to Jesus, and being patient with them as we grow.*
>
> *It's one thing to show mercy to believers who fall, reaching out to them with compassion and gently leading them back to restoration.*

It's one thing to preach against legalism, which I define as externally imposed religion, meaning, laws without love, rules without relationship, and standards without a Savior.

And it's one thing to extol God's grace, recognizing that He loves on our good days and our bad days and that our relationship with Jesus is not measured by our latest spiritual accomplishment.

But it's another thing entirely to be polluted by the world in the name of liberty and to exalt the flesh in the name of freedom.

Paul warned about this plainly, writing, "For you were called to freedom, brothers. Only do not use your freedom as an opportunity for the flesh, but through love serve one another.(Galatians 5:13)"[53]

IS THERE EVIDENCE OF CHRIST IN THE LIVES OF YOUR CHURCH MEMBERS?

In the Great Commission, we are called to make disciples who obey what Christ commanded.[54]

The question for pastors is not, *Are people getting baptized?* or *Are we doing good things collectively as a group?* or *Is Sunday attendance up?*. The question is, *Are marks of Christlikeness evident in the individual lives of the members of my church?*

If you are a pastor or church leader, before you answer, what do you consider evidence of Christlikeness in your members?

- Do they exhibit fervent, committed, passionate love for God as Jesus described? (Matthew 22:37)
- Do they hunger to learn the Scripture? (1 Peter 2:2)
- Are they identifying and overcoming patterns of sin in their life? (1 John 2:14)
- Do they exhibit sacrificial love for others—loving, forgiving, and serving the way Jesus did, even to people who do not deserve it? (Matthew 22, 38; Philippians 2:5–11)
- Do they desire to share the Good News with other people? Do they live as missionaries, responding to whatever God asks of them? Do they exhibit personal responsibility for fulfilling the Great Commission? (Matthew 28:18–20, John 15:16, 2 Corinthians 5:14–20)
- Is Christianity just something they say they believe? Are their priorities, resources, time, and energy lined up around it, or are they preoccupied with the pleasures of this world? (Mark 4:19)

Today's Christianity is inundated with pastors, leaders, and church members trying to give everyone assurance of their salvation. Where are those who will admonish people to examine themselves, to see if Christ is truly among them, to see if they pass the test of genuine faith, even as the Apostle Paul did?[55] The sad reality is, many people do not have evidence of a saving faith.

Continually overemphasizing the love of God and the individual's worth can inadvertently communicate to people that they are saved because they are loveable. They then come to church, feel emotional or positive about God, and leave feeling no need to change.

In a study of more than 250,000 congregants, Hawkins and Parkinson discovered a continuum of spiritual growth evident in the lives of those they surveyed. It ranged from exploring Christ, to growing in Christ, to becoming close to Christ, and finally to living a Christ-centered life. In short, they measured spiritual growth—Christlikeness—by the ways in which people loved God and loved others.[56]

The Christian life is not just about being forgiven; we live new lives. Salvation does not mean we have a license to sin. Grace does not enable us to do what we want and be assured of our salvation.

> *What then? Shall we sin because we are not under law but under grace? May it never be! Romans 6:15 NLT*

Grace changes us. It transforms us.

> *Therefore, if anyone is in Christ, the new creation has come: The old has gone, the new is here! 2 Corinthians 5:17 NLT*

We should weep with repentance and gratitude that "He who knew no sin became sin for us".[57] That God "laid on Him the iniquity of us all".[58] It should break our hearts that our sin put

Jesus through pain. This is "Godly sorrow" that "brings repentance that leads to salvation".[59]

Many today treat the grace of God with arrogant self-entitlement, which leads to trampling the blood of Jesus underfoot and crucifying the Son of God anew, insulting the Spirit of grace.[60] We can make people so comfortable that they are never confronted with the message of sin and repentance. We must challenge people to regularly evaluate themselves for evidence of Christ in their lives.

> *Test yourselves to see if you are in the faith; examine yourselves! Or do you not recognize this about yourselves, that Jesus Christ is in you—unless indeed you fail the test?*
> 2 Corinthians 13:5 NASB

Overcoming sinful desires is a process and requires cooperation with the Holy Spirit. Sweet and Viola describe what happens when the supremacy of Christ is returned to the church:

> *It means that church members will know their Lord better than they know their church programs. It means that Jesus will get airplay in their conversations. It means His melody will resound through their actions and reverberate in their attitudes.*[61]

Many are hesitant at the thought of evaluating others for signs of spiritual growth. But the study of Scripture and church history reveals that Jesus, the apostles, and the early church all looked for evidence of Christlikeness in the lives of Christ followers.

ASSESSING FOR GROWTH

Jesus' practice. Jesus taught that the fruit a person bears—that is, their outward behavior—is evidence of their heart.

> *Beware of false prophets who come disguised as harmless sheep but are really vicious wolves. You can identify them by their fruit, that is, by the way they act. Can you pick grapes from thornbushes, or figs from thistles? . . . A good tree can't produce bad fruit, and a bad tree can't produce good fruit.*
> *Matthew 7:15-16,18 NLT*

Believers bear fruit. Spiritual fruit is inward change with an outward manifestation. It is the work of the Spirit transforming one's character that produces a testimony to the world, both through action and deed, that Christ is at work in the person.[62] We should not accept at face value that everyone who says they are of Christ truly are. An examination of their life over time is more telling.

> *In the same way, let your light shine before others, that they may see your good deeds and glorify your Father in heaven. Mathew 5:16*

To be clear, works *do not produce salvation*; however, salvation produces works—obedient living.

> *For it is by grace you have been saved, through faith—and this is not from yourselves, it is the gift of God—not by works, so that no one can boast. <u>For we are God's handiwork, created in Christ Jesus to do good works</u>, which God prepared in advance for us to do. Ephesians 2:8-10 (emphasis added)*
>
> *You did not choose me, but I chose you and appointed you so that you might go and bear fruit—fruit that will last—and so that whatever you ask in my name the Father will give you. John 15:16*

The first Church's practice. The New Testament writers, under the inspiration of the Holy Spirit, instructed the church to judge itself. Notice the following instruction from the Apostle Paul:

> *It isn't my responsibility to judge outsiders, but it certainly is your responsibility to judge those inside the church who are sinning. God will judge those on the outside; but as the Scriptures say, "You must remove the evil person from among you." 1 Corinthians 5:12-13 NLT*

While we are to preach the truth about sin and warn *everyone* of its consequences, we cannot hold an *unbeliever* accountable to live as a Christian. The world cannot be expected to honor the truth because they have not surrendered to Jesus and do not have His Spirit living in them, to change them.

However, there *are* appropriate times for a believer to point out the faults of another believer and challenge them to change, to hold other believers accountable to God's Word. Many believers incorrectly assume that it is wrong to tell other Christians they are doing something wrong, because that would be "judging" them. The previous passage clearly states, though, that we have this responsibility. To judge means *"to pronounce an opinion concerning right and wrong."*[63] The church must teach what is right and wrong according to the truth of the Word of God. The Apostle Paul gave this instruction:

> *Brothers and sisters, if someone is caught in a sin, you who live by the Spirit should restore that person gently. But watch yourselves, or you also may be tempted. Galatians 6:1*

How can you fulfill the obligation to restore your fellow Christian to the right path if you are not allowed to tell them that they sinned in the first place? We should all expect and value loving correction from more mature believers.

The early Church's practice. Early church documents explain that for a span of three years, early church leaders instructed and inspected the lives of potential Christians to see if there was evidence of Christ in them. This was done before baptizing and receiving them into church fellowship. Leaders carefully looked for the character and the compassion of Christ in the lives of new converts.[64]

While this level of scrutiny before baptism might seem a bit extreme, one lesson can be learned. The early church believed that those who are born of Christ bear the character of Christ. They were careful to guard the fellowship against those who professed faith in Christ but whose lives bore no marks of His transforming presence.

Expecting to see Christlikeness in church members is not a license to become self-righteous and belittling to others. Scripture is clear, we must be careful to remove the beam from our own eyes before we help our brother with the speck in his eye.[65] It commands us to gently restore people who have fallen, acknowledging it could be us next time.[66] But nevertheless, we have an obligation to warn those who are straying from the truth and protect the sheep from wolves in sheep's clothing.[67]

Considering the practice of Jesus, the apostles, and the early church, and contrasting the power of God they experienced with what most churches experience today, perhaps we should reevaluate our church membership. After all, people can like your church, but have no interest in Christ.

CONFRONT THE WEEKEND CROWD WITH THE COST OF DISCIPLESHIP

Many models of church growth today recommend preaching a message tailored to the Sunday crowd, one not as focused on following Christ as what would be preached to the committed Christian "core" some other point in the week. There is an inherent flaw in this thinking. If people regularly attend your church, they are typically considered part of the fellowship of believers, particularly if they have confessed faith in Jesus. Many times they're not engaged with anything but the Sunday morning service, so they're not confronted with the real cost of discipleship. Jesus did not reserve this teaching for people who were three steps in. It was the first ask He made.

We should always keep an open seat at a table for those who are curious about Jesus—skeptical, and not yet believing. Making every effort to help the unbeliever understand the Gospel is a paramount function of the church. However, great care must be exercised to guard the fellowship of believers. We must be careful not to lead unbelievers to think they are saved because they like our church or are considered part of it. In doing so, we could very well be confirming the damning faith we are warned about.

A Jesus-centered church will not elevate your sin or beat you up over it, but neither will it ignore or make excuses for it. It will support you and help you overcome it!

Chapter Seven
Jesus-Centered Gatherings

When Jesus returns to the supreme place in His Church, our worship services will also center around Him. The issue will no longer be young vs. old, traditional vs. contemporary, believer vs. lost, member vs. visitor. It will no longer be a preoccupation with certain preaching, teaching, and music styles. It will no longer be a fascination with gifts, charisma, or personalities—whether in others or yourself.

Jesus will become our focal point. Our preoccupation. Our fascination.

We gather to worship and experience Christ. He promised that if we do this in His Name, He will be present.[68] He will speak to us, commune with us, touch us, heal us, and free us. We typically make gatherings, at best, about things that are second rate to the presence of Jesus and are, at worst, idols that completely shroud us from experiencing Him.

In August of 2021, along with billions around the world, I witnessed news coverage of the Taliban taking over Afghanistan. It was a turbulent and sometimes terrifying reality that we all had to reckon with. It was just the latest of countless events throughout the course of human history that emphasize the need for a Savior.

Amidst this horrific situation, there were so many reports of Christians gathering with each other, praying, worshiping, and communing in secret. And this decision, every single time, was a life-or-death decision for them. After the initial coup, the news shifted to Christians being murdered daily—Afghani believers who were pulled from their homes and meeting places and killed mercilessly for claiming that Jesus is Lord. And yet, they still gather as the family of Jesus. The Western Church can never comprehend this risk.

I experienced powerful worship during one Wednesday prayer service at the church I was shepherding at the time. The presence of Christ was real, but I couldn't help but wonder, *Why would people in the persecuted church risk their lives to gather?*

So many Western Christians exist in this mindset: *I can love the Lord at home. I wouldn't risk dying to gather with other believers. It wouldn't be necessary.* Or, *If my relationship with God is personal, why should I prioritize being part of a church? I can grow with God on my own?* Western Christianity holds a desperately flawed paradigm in believing that the church community is optional.

And, let's face it, take the best church service—the most amazing production, most powerful worship, most moving message. These things are great and important, but they're not worth risking your life over.

What is worth the risk when these persecuted Christians are without abundant resources, cushy programs, and comfortable, safe places of worship? What makes gathering to Christians in persecution *so incredibly important* that they would risk death to do it?

Is it possible that they *truly* experience Jesus when they gather? If so, *that* is worth dying for.

> *For where two or three are gathered in my name, there am I among them.*
> *Matthew 18:20 ESV*

This verse should wake us up to a new reality. This isn't just a go-to verse to quote when attendance is low. It means that even if just a few followers gather, Jesus is there. It's not *like* He is there. He isn't metaphorically there. He *is* there. This also infers that Jesus promised to show up differently when people are gathered than when they encounter Him alone.

If Jesus is present when we gather, our first question should be, "What does Jesus want out of this gathering?" We must be crystal clear when discerning this. It is more involved and more important than a thirty-second circle prayer before a creative planning meeting.

The problem is not creativity or modern teaching, worship, and church experiences. It is when we spend more time on planning and preparing than we do seeking the heart and will of Jesus. If this is the case, something is wildly out of balance.

Church leaders must focus on ensuring that the very real power of Jesus is present in their gatherings. If we do this, then many of the things we strive for and stress over will stop mattering so much. The spiritually hungry won't care as much because they will be receiving what they need, not just receiving something that simply entertains their senses for an hour on Sunday. Francis Chan warns:

> *The benchmark of success in church services has become more about attendance than the movement of the Holy Spirit. The "entertainment" model of church was largely adopted in the 1980s and '90s and while it alleviated some of our boredom for a couple of hours a week, it filled our churches with self-focused consumers rather than self-sacrificing servants attuned to the Holy Spirit.* [69]

Some say, "It doesn't matter why people come to our church services, as long as they come and hear the message." Be cautious with this attitude.

If people are coming or staying for any other reason than to seek to understand or experience Christ, is it truly a valid reason? Remember, what attracts people keeps people. If they are not immediately immersed in an environment of connecting with Jesus and receiving His message, they will most likely not take that step later. You will likely feel compelled to continue to create environments that appeal to their senses rather than their spirits.

Practically speaking, music and teaching styles must be selected. We should make newcomers feel welcome, and we should be sensitive to diverse generations and cultures, as well as uninformed unbelievers in the room. After all, Christlikeness isn't selfish, demanding, and elitist—whether you are young or old. But if we make Christ the focal point of our gatherings, the spirit with which we address many of these things will change. Rather than fighting about which group's needs will take priority, we will discern and meet His desires.

Christ-centered worship. Churches of all styles and denominations are at risk of creating worship experiences that do not put Christ at the center. Through primarily unspoken cues, people come to watch what a few worship leaders at the front are doing. Traditional and contemporary churches of all streams of doctrine and practice are guilty of this.

A large part of the Christian worship experience involves music. But when the focus shifts to the exaltation of Christ, musical styles become less important. We often put far too much emphasis on music in the church, while neglecting the other biblical expressions of worship such as praying, kneeling, taking communion, lifting our hands, or bowing before the Lord. Not to mention various other arts that can be used as valid, creative expressions of worship to the master Creator of all things. When we gather for the presence of Jesus, we will long to express love to Him through every means possible.

Prayer-driven worship. When Jesus is at the center, the church becomes a house of prayer once again. Yes, there is time for preaching, teaching, worship, fellowship, and outreach. But red-hot passionate prayer becomes the central aspect of the church and its gathering. Why? Because prayer is communion with Jesus. People once again learn to love God with all their heart, soul, and mind. Prayer is not just another thing we do; it is the *central* thing we do. The thing from which everything else flows. He is present when we gather in His Name, and we will desire to commune with Him.

When Christ is at the center of a gathering, it is not uncommon for worship services to be equally led by worship and prayer leaders. The worship leaders help us minister to the heart of God, and the prayer leaders help us petition the throne of God with prayers and intercession.

My personal faith story is filled with people of passionate prayer. Both in their personal lives and at the pre-service altars of the church, you could hear desperate prayers of the saints ringing out as they petitioned God to move in their midst with His power. I find it unfortunate that many praying people from past generations fought and lost the "music/worship" wars in church, while they should have been fighting prayer wars. The stance should have been, "Whatever our music might sound like is negotiable, as long as we don't lose the practice of prayer in our gatherings." Now, too often, the skills, charisma, and personalities of worship leaders and preachers replace the power of God that only comes through prayer. *(Refer to Appendix 1 for suggestions on how to return prayer to its central place in your church.)*

The return to Holy Communion. Receiving the sacrament of Communion was a primary focus of the gatherings of the early Church, and much of the Church throughout history. To relegate this to an occasional event strips the Church from receiving Jesus through this sacrament. Jesus was clear when He said, "This bread is my body, this cup is my blood" (1 Corinthians 11:23-25).

The very real presence of Jesus inhabits the sacraments.

A return to repentance will fill our gatherings as we turn our attention to the cross every week and examine our lives, confessing sin to the Lord before receiving Communion. Believers and nonbelievers will experience the grace and implications of the Gospel every time the Church comes to the Table of the Lord.

Welcoming unbelievers into Christ's presence. Unbelievers should be welcomed to experience and learn about Jesus. Who He is. What He should mean to them. What He says about life. But they should also encounter Christ's presence, words, and power through our church and its gatherings.

Yes, we should be sensitive to those present who don't know Jesus. We should slow down to explain things to those who have little biblical knowledge. That's just smart. But sensitivity to the lost does not mean *censorship* for the lost. Our goal should not be to entertain them with good worship or impress them with a fiery or feel-good preacher. Our primary purpose should be to teach them about Jesus and give them an opportunity to experience Him.

Believers and seekers alike should gather knowing that they will experience Jesus and hear what He is saying about their lives. They should gather to live out Jesus' mission together as a family. It is truly about Him and what He desires of them.

Because He is present:
>We will worship Him.
>We will be called to repentance.
>His words will be taught.
>We will long for His power to work in the lives of everyone in the room.

And Jesus will draw all men to the Father as He is lifted up (John 12:32).

Chapter Eight
Jesus-Centered Preaching

I grew up in a home where reading was a pastime. We didn't have a TV, so I spent tens of thousands of hours as a child reading. I spent much of that time reading biblical storybooks, reading bible commentary for youth, and reading the Bible itself. By the age of twelve, I had read through the entirety of the Bible for the first time—I still have the award plaque to prove it!

And I also grew up spending a lot of time listening to numerous preachers speak and teach. When I compared what I was hearing to the ample personal time I had spent reading and studying, something didn't quite line up. I always felt something was off. Not necessarily all wrong, but off. Incomplete. Missing something.

I had heard thousands of sermons and lessons from a variety of Christian traditions.

I heard:
> About the Bible.
> About the heroes from the Bible.
> About the Church.
> About men and the roles they were to play in life and Church.
> About women and what women should or shouldn't wear, and what role they could or could not play in life and Church
> About the "End Time" and the Tribulation.
> About the judgment of God.
> About the Holy Spirit.
> About gifts of the Holy Spirit.
> And the list goes on and on.

And I also heard a lot of teachings about Jesus— who He was, what He did, and His return. And these are all critical things.

But one day, after having been in ministry myself for fifteen years, it hit me like a ton of bricks.

It occurred to me that while the Church spends a lot of time teaching about a variety of topics from the Bible, even about Jesus Himself, we rarely actually teach the topics that Jesus taught or emphasize the things Jesus emphasized. His teachings are not often valued at the level that Scripture commands.

We must understand that Jesus did not just come to die; He came to say something as well.

> *But he said, "I must proclaim the good news of the kingdom of God to the other towns also, because that is why I was sent. Luke 4:43*

Notice the following:

> *Long ago, at many times and in many ways, God spoke to our fathers by the prophets, but in these last days he has spoken to us by his Son, whom he appointed the heir of all things . . . He is the radiance of the glory of God and the exact imprint of his nature, and he upholds the universe by the word of his power. Hebrews 1:1-3*

Jesus came to say something, and He took His teachings—His words—very serious:

- Heaven and earth will pass away, but my <u>words</u> will never pass away. Matthew 24:35

- If anyone is ashamed of me and <u>my words</u> in this adulterous and sinful generation, the Son of Man will be ashamed of him when he comes in his Father's glory with the holy angels." Mark 8:38

- He replied, "My mother and brothers are those who <u>hear God's word and put it into practice</u>." Luke 8:21

- It is the Spirit who gives life; the flesh is no help at all. The _words that I have spoken_ to you are spirit and life. John 6:63 ESV

- Jesus replied, "If I glorify myself, my glory means nothing. My Father, whom you claim as your God, is the one who glorifies me. Though you do not know him, I know him. If I said I did not, I would be a liar like you, but _I do know him and keep his word._ John 8:54-55

- There is a judge for the one who rejects me and does not accept my words; the very words I have spoken will condemn them at the last day. For I did not speak on my own, but _the Father who sent me commanded me to say all that I have spoken_. John 12:48-49

- Anyone who does not love me will not obey my teaching. These _words you hear are not my own_; they belong to the Father who sent me. John 14:24

- You are already clean because of _the word_ I have spoken to you. John 15:3

- For I gave them _the words you gave me_ and they accepted them. They knew with certainty that I came from you, and they believed that you sent me. John 17:8

- Sanctify them by the truth; _your word is truth_. John 17:17

- But the Advocate, the Holy Spirit, whom the Father will send in my name, will teach you all things and will remind you of everything I have said to you. John 14:26

Furthermore, Jesus expected His followers to obey His teachings

> *Why do you call me, 'Lord, Lord,' and do not do what I say? Luke 6:46*
>
> *Therefore everyone who hears these words of mine and puts them into practice is like a wise man who built his house on the rock. Matthew 7:24*

Jesus directed His first followers to make new disciples and teach the new followers to obey everything He had taught them.

> *Then Jesus came to them and said, "All authority in heaven and on earth has been given to me. Therefore go and make disciples of all nations, baptizing them in the name of the Father and of the Son and of the Holy Spirit, and teaching them to obey everything I have commanded you. And surely I am with you always, to the very end of the age." Matthew 28:18-20*

The first believers knew that Jesus' words led to life, so they devoted themselves to His teachings.

> *Simon Peter answered him, "Lord, to whom shall we go? You have the words of eternal life. John 6:68*

Remember a Christian is becoming like Christ. We are His disciples. Meaning we are students of His life and teachings.

But in much of today's popular Christianity, devotion and obedience to Jesus' teachings seem optional. Even in many of the churches that claim to be "teaching" churches or "word" churches, they will study all over the Bible, yet somehow conveniently side-step Jesus' teachings.

Now, of course, we would never say that we think Jesus' teachings are optional, but what do our daily actions say?

As preachers and teacher of the gospel, we must return Christ and His message to the center of all that we speak, teach, and communicate. Sweet and Viola explain the implications of understanding the supremacy of Christ in our preaching:

> *If a person is truly inspired by the Spirit of God when he or she is speaking, that individual's message will be Christ. . . . Why? Because the Spirit is totally occupied with Christ . . . when someone is teaching from the Scriptures—and being true to the Word of God—that teacher will unveil Christ through the text… Why? Because*

> *the Scriptures are completely occupied with Christ.*
>
> *Consequently, those who do not present Christ when they minister not only miss a note, but they play the wrong tune. The tragedy of our time is that countless preachers, teachers, even healers are giving dozens of sermons, lectures, and messages, relegating Jesus to little more than a footnote or a flourish to some other subject. . . . What is lacking is a groundbreaking revelation of Christ that boggles the mind and enraptures the heart.*[70]

Beginning with the Gospels and continuing through the other books of the New Testament, we see that Jesus came to reconcile the world back to God—to make all things new. He is the exact representation of God—the visible image of an invisible God. Therefore, He has most clearly revealed God's character to us.

Through Jesus' death and resurrection, all things necessary for our salvation and reconciliation with God are fulfilled. By giving us His Holy Spirit, everything we need to live in God's will is made available. But understand that the will of God is defined by Jesus' life and teachings.

The Christian life is more than just behavior modification; it is spiritual transformation. It is the old becoming new. It is not enough to make some good points and add scriptures for support. Jesus must saturate our preaching.

We must not just talk about Jesus; we must also see a return to preaching the *message* of Jesus. Talking about the things Jesus talked about.

THE MESSAGE OF JESUS

The teachings of Christ—His values, His words, His principles—must be emphasized in our preaching, regardless of who it offends. It is His message that leads to life. To preach anything less is preaching death. We were instructed to not only make disciples of Jesus, but also teach them to obey everything He commanded. In other words, we must teach the gospels—the words "in red."[71]

This includes the following:

- The cost as well as the benefits of following Him
- Denial of self; living to honor God and serve others
- Placing Him in the supreme place in our lives
- Blessed are the pure in heart, the poor in spirit, the meek, the persecuted
- Praying for those who misuse us; blessing those who curse us
- Caring for the least among us
- Responsibly stewarding money and resources entrusted to us
- Dealing with our heart and motives (e.g., lust, hate) not just the externals (e.g., adultery, murder)
- Trusting God to care for His children
- The Kingdom of God
- Heaven and Hell
- And a myriad of other themes contained in the gospels

This emphasis on the teachings of Christ and His apostles does not discredit other scripture as less inspired or true. After all, it was the Spirit of Jesus—the Holy Spirit—that spoke through the prophets. It simply means that the Son has most clearly communicated God's desires for us.

Hebrew Scriptures (the Old Testament) point forward to Jesus. New Testament letters point back to Jesus. *He is the center of it all.*

THE PRESENT POWER OF JESUS IN OUR PREACHING

Preaching Christ-centered messages will often frustrate the efforts of those trying to live out His teachings through their own power. Any attempt to do so without His presence is futile. Sweet and Viola remind us of this:

> *Jesus cannot be separated from His teachings. Aristotle said to his disciples, "Follow my teachings." Socrates likewise said to his disciples, "Follow my teachings." Buddha said to his disciples, "Follow my meditations." Confucius said to his disciples, "Follow my sayings." And Muhammad said to his disciples, "Follow my noble pillars." But Jesus says to His disciples, "Follow Me."*

> *In all the religions and philosophies of the world, a follower can follow the teachings of its founder without having a relationship with that founder. But not so with Jesus Christ. The teachings of Jesus cannot be separated from*

Jesus Himself. Christ is still alive, and He embodies His teachings.[72]

To live as Christ did, we must allow His power to live through us. This means our preaching should routinely result in altars full of people seeking salvation and deliverance from the power of sin and experiencing the overcoming victory of Christ in their life. Then we must teach people new ways to think through repentance and the renewing of their minds. Ways that honor God and fulfill the purpose they were made for.

Preachers and teachers, ask yourselves this: *Do I spend as much time in prayer seeking the power and demonstration of the Holy Spirit's influence in my message as I do researching and crafting the words and creative elements I will employ?*

Do we believe the Holy Spirit can do something sovereign in our services, or does He only work through the words we speak, or the gifts of the hospitality team, worship leaders, and teachers?

This is not an excuse for sloppy preaching, a lack of study, or due diligence and preparation in speaking to God's people. This is a call to pray for the Holy Spirit to bring conviction and power when we preach. But be warned—if people are not on fire for Jesus, they will reject a challenging message and want to go where they only feel good or encouraged. My question is, *Encouraged to do what?* Encouraged to live life the way you want, while people around you are dying and going to hell?

If the only message that people hear is a feel-good motivational speech, with no focus on scriptural correction and Holy Spirit empowerment, they will be unequipped and powerless when it really counts. When all hell breaks loose, will we have the power to prevail?

May Jesus return to the supreme place that He was meant to occupy in our teaching and preaching.

Chapter Nine
Jesus-Centered Outreach

As a young pastor, I remember being completely intrigued by Pastor Steve Sjogren's description of servant evangelism at Vineyard Cincinnati Church. I was enthralled and excited to build a culture of serving in my church that resembled his. And there's absolutely nothing wrong with creatively, passionately meeting the needs of people in your community.

We soon discovered, though, that issues began to arise when believers were more excited about meeting people's needs than they were concerned with their relationship with Jesus. It's dangerous if we are primarily rallying around serving, rather than gathering for the presence of Jesus.

If we are not first violently in love with Jesus, we will unknowingly lead people to the wrong thing. Rather than teaching others to passionately follow Him, we could be teaching them excitement about ministry in His name, absent from ever truly knowing Him. And that is dangerously deceptive.

> *On that day many will say to me, "Lord, Lord, did we not prophesy in your name, and cast out demons in your name, and do many mighty works in your name?" 23 And then will I declare to them, "I never knew you." Matthew 7:22-23 ESV*

Look at this stiff rebuke by Jesus to the Pharisees:

> *For you travel land and sea to win one proselyte, and when he is won, you make him twice as much a son of hell as yourselves. Matthew 23:15 NKJV*

That's very strong language from Jesus.

The issue gets worse when we begin to think that serving the humanitarian needs of the world is the primary mission of the church. We serve because we are Christians, "because He first loved us,"[73] because we love our neighbor as we love ourselves.[74] We serve because He commanded us to. We serve because we are meeting other's needs as if we are meeting His.[75] But our central *mission* is to preach the Gospel to all people and reconcile the world to God.[76] We do not necessarily have to give an altar call every time we give someone a cup of water, but we should certainly tell them the love for Jesus is motivating us to give that cup. He must be the undeniable motive behind our serving and outreach.

It requires constant evaluation to make sure we're not drifting from Jesus. This is tough. The truth is, most people simply do not want to take time for hard conversations and analysis. Particularly when there are so many needs in the world, and so few people meeting them.

CODEPENDENT OUTREACH

Love for people is often what moves us to show love to them. And we should love others. But if we only preach to or serve others when we love them or feel like they deserve it, our preaching and serving is at risk of ending when we are upset with them. If we preach the Gospel because we love Jesus, we are motivated to continue despite people's responses.

If you get very excited about the "love for people" message, but are not burning red-hot for Jesus, you are dangerous—and not in a good way. In fact, just the opposite. This posture can make you a fatal threat to His mission.

Why would I use such strong language?

Sometimes we can operate out of codependency. It's possible to have a savior complex, where we feel it is our job to save, love, and fix everyone—meaning we must keep everyone happy at all costs. It is dangerous because we can intervene when the Holy Spirit is uncomfortably challenging people to change. It's very important that we do not confuse the spiritual gift of mercy—having compassion for people—with codependency.

The teachings of Jesus may offend a person living in sin, but there is hope their soul may be saved from hell. If we become more angry at the message and messenger than heartbroken over the potential that the offended person we love may end up in hell, then we are glorifying that person over God. We are more concerned about their feelings and what they will think about us if we share Jesus' teaching than we are with offending God.

If you suffer from these codependent traits and do not burn for the Lord, you may set yourself up as an ally for lukewarm people as He turns up the heat in church. When people begin experiencing the Lord's conviction and power, they can become confused or angry. When this happens, a codependent person may undermine the church elders and the Holy Spirit's work by listening to and trying to appease the disgruntled, just as Absalom undermined King David's authority (see 2 Samuel 15-18).

If you are overly fixated on people rather than Jesus, it is very likely that on a conscious or unconscious level, your salvation is tied to your works. You might define yourself by the work you do in ministry and the impact you are making in the community. You begin truly believing that you are expressing Christ's love, following His will because you are staying busy. But like the Ephesian church, something other than red-hot love for Jesus is motivating your service. You may forget that works of service for people should flow from your love for God; they do not earn His love.

With codependent behavior, identity can be defined by what you are doing for others and the attention you get from serving, not from simply knowing who you are. You are a child of God. Remember that the Holy Spirit expresses and manifests Himself through our spiritual gifts. He will not accommodate people in their sin. Codependency will.

OUTREACH IS ABOUT JESUS

Often, we see outreach as a way to build our church, but evangelism isn't about our church or even the lost. It is about Jesus and the price He paid, and the right He earned for all the world to know about Him.

Remember our message: There is a God who made the world and loves the world. There is a world that rejected the God that made them and loves them, and we are all in danger of eternal separation from Him because of our sin. Motivated by His love for the world, Jesus came and died for us to redeem us back to Himself. He has earned the right for every person in the world to know who He is and what He has done for them.

Unbelievers might very well be attracted to your church because of the love it expressed by meeting physical and emotional needs in the community. But if we are not meeting needs in the name of Jesus, with the message of Jesus, pointing people to Jesus, then we are at risk of developing disciples of something other than Jesus. Outreach is not meant to create an interest in church, but an interest in Him.

If we are more needs-focused than Christ-focused, we are in danger of creating consumers who think the church exists to serve them instead of Him. The focus and motivation of outreach should be Christ's love.

If you serve because of your love for Jesus, because He has asked you to, you will be excited to tell people about Him as you serve them. You will point any gratitude that they express toward Jesus, thanking Him for sending you to them. This is not a suggestion to refuse to help someone unless they get "saved" first. It is a reminder that we meet needs out of love for Jesus, and He should be shared as we serve!

SHARE THE GOSPEL

Some will say, "I will just show the love of God to people without actually talking about it with them. They will be able to see Christ by my actions." The following quote is often used to support this belief: "Preach wherever you go, and when necessary use words." It is often attributed to St. Francis of Assisi. However, no record exists that he said this. He preached with words wherever he went.[77]

This idea of preaching without words is good in sentiment only. Scripture is clear that we must tell people about the Good News of Jesus. Our actions can certainly credit or discredit that news, but good actions alone can never replace preaching the Gospel to an unsaved, lost world.

Logically, if a person does not know about Jesus—and indeed many have *never* heard about Jesus or have a narrow or twisted view of Him—they will never know that He motivates your attitude or actions unless you tell them. They might notice that you are different from others, but you must be ready to explain why you are different.

> *Instead, you must worship Christ as Lord of your life. And if someone asks about your Christian hope, always be ready to explain it.*
> *1 Peter 3:15 NLT*

People must know about Jesus and His love. They must know who He is and what He came to earth to do. They can only know that if you tell them.

> *How, then, can they call on the one they have not believed in? And how can they believe in the one of whom they have not heard? And how can they hear without someone preaching to them? Romans 10:14*

Preaching the Good News does not only refer to Bible teaching and training by teaching pastors and preachers. The word preach means "to proclaim openly . . . something which has been done."[78] Jesus commands every disciple to proclaim what He has done.

> *He said to them, "Go into all the world and preach the gospel to all creation." Mark 16:15*

Some people are gifted by God with evangelism. They are very effective at proclaiming the Gospel and bringing people to faith in Jesus. However, this does not exempt other disciples from this task. We are all called to do the work of an evangelist, sharing His Good News.[79]

We might not all stand in front of large groups or in public forums, but we can all share the Gospel with *someone*. Our current level of discomfort with speaking it cannot replace the Great Commission given by Jesus to go into all the world and make disciples.

We must also be clear about the message we preach. When you offer salvation, you are asking a person to repent and submit to the Lordship of Jesus. In doing so, they will be saved from their sin and spiritually reborn as a child of God. They will then live their lives as a disciple of Jesus—doing the will of God with Jesus as their Lord and teacher—and will spend eternity with Him. The Holy Spirit will give them assurance of their rebirth, which will be evidenced by the fruit of a changed life.

Chapter Ten
Jesus-Centered Ministry

When we make it all about Jesus, our motivation for Christian ministry changes. Ministry opportunities are no longer about us. We live our lives listening to Him, and then responding to and doing what He desires.

Over the course of a lifetime of pastoring, I have had countless people ask me, *"What does God want from me? What is my place in the church?"*

It is crucial to understand, first and foremost, our place is at the feet of Jesus in prayer and worship, both in private and corporately with spiritual brothers and sisters. Giving Him love. Learning His heart. Feeling His desires. Hearing His direction. We were made by Him, for Him (Colossians 1:16).

Remember Mary, pouring out all she had on His feet. Judas scolded her, using Jesus' own teaching to care for the poor to discourage her extravagant, costly worship. Jesus corrected him. There's a time to serve the poor, but our first place is at His feet, in communion with Him.[80] When we get this right, He will show us what He desires from us.

We must be cautious about continuous doing. Doing for the Lord can become an idol. When He tells you to wait and sit at His feet, and you can't because you're busy doing for Him, your zeal to serve is probably motivated by something other than honoring Him. That's a tough truth to hear and even tougher to admit.

At times, the better choice is sitting at His feet, communing with Him, listening to Him. At other times, Jesus was in such a hurry that people couldn't say goodbye to friends or attend funerals. They had to move right then.[81] So, which response is right? The answer is, whatever Jesus desires in the moment. He is the center of our lives, ministry, and service. Not ourselves.

FALSE MOTIVATIONS FOR SERVING

The opinion of others. Remember, your assignment is based on doing what God desires. It is not based on the response or desire of people. One of Jesus' first sermons resulted in the listeners trying to throw him off a cliff.[82] Talk about rejection! What's even more interesting is what happened next: He went into a new town and began preaching again. Now, that in itself is a miracle. Many of us would not have gotten over the feelings of failure and self-pity to try again. But Jesus did—and they loved Him. They loved Him so much that when He attempted to leave a few days later, they begged Him to stay. His response was, "I have to go preach to the other towns, for that's why I was sent" (Luke 4:43, my paraphrase). Truthfully, a lot of us would never have left that town. *"They love me! I've found my people!"* would have been our response.

But Jesus was neither swayed by the *rejection* nor the *approval* of others. He only did what He saw His Father doing. His assignment came solely from the Father's will, not people's reactions. How did He know the Father so well? Deep communion with Him.

Personal ambition. Personal ambition is often disguised in the "sheep's coat" of ministry. In reality, it is a wolf that will destroy you and others.

It can be difficult to discern when you are being fueled by personal ambition—the need to be recognized, or even the need to accomplish—rather than directed by Jesus' requests. It's easy to justify most ministry activities by quoting Scripture that supports your behavior in the moment. Remember Judas' treatment of Mary?

Has Jesus asked you to minister, or is your ministry fulfilling a need in you that should be fulfilled through relationship with Him? Never forget, Jesus is not a shortcut to filling a sinful need for narcissistic satisfaction, regardless of how many churches will exploit those desires to get what they want from you.

TARRY FOR POWER

As you begin to spend time tarrying in prayer at His feet, He will give you assignments as you are ready. But before these, and more important than them, He desires a relationship, or communion, with you. At times He will tell you to slow down and wait before you engage in ministry.

Communion is "the sharing or exchanging of intimate thoughts and feelings, especially when the exchange is on a mental or spiritual level."[83] It is both talking with, listening to, and being with Him. If you are in a conversation where you have questions, but all you do is talk, how can you expect to hear any answers? It is impossible to hear the voice of God if you only talk in prayer. It is a give-and-take avenue of communication. He talks, you listen. You talk, He listens.

Sometimes you must settle yourself to hear the voice of God. We often need to simply sit and be in the silence. God will reveal things in these times of quiet that we don't allow Him to when we constantly talk, reason, beg, question, and explain while we pray.

Prayer should not be a monologue that God listens to as the audience of a melodramatic performance. Prayer *can* be a dialogue between parent and child, where they both listen and talk. It can be a deep dive where we explore the depths of Him by settling and "soaking" in the transcendent waters of His presence. It can be a cinematic marathon where we binge-watch visions with Him for hours.

No matter what it is, it starts with devotion to Jesus-centered prayer. There are no shortcuts to this. You have to learn to tarry.

> *Behold, I send the Promise of My Father upon you; but <u>tarry</u> in the city of Jerusalem until you*

> *are endued with power from on high. Luke 24:49 NKJV (emphasis added)*

Tarry (from the Greek word *kathizo*) means "to make to sit down, to have fixed one's abode, to dwell."[84] This denotes being relaxed and settled. For example, Scripture says that Jesus would sit down—*kathizo*—and teach people, sometimes for days. He was not in a hurry.[85]

It's interesting that the final time in His earthly life He told them to tarry with Him was in the Garden of Gethsemane, right before His execution. "Could you not [tarry] in prayer with me one hour?" He asked them as He woke them from sleep.[86] After his resurrection, He picked up with them right where he left off. He told them to return to Jerusalem to tarry—settle down and wait—for power. The last time they were there, they were running out of the city, denying Him, fleeing for their lives as He was being executed.

Jesus promised that after they waited, they would be baptized—*baptizo*—with power. This particular word refers to a pickling process, a slow fermentation to the point that a cucumber comes out a pickle—its very nature is changed.[87] It requires time and discipline, and humans, by very nature, fight against discipline. People may resist the idea of tarrying for the baptism of the Holy Spirit until they have experienced it firsthand. There are no shortcuts to communion. You have to do your time.

But time spent in the presence of Jesus is not wasted. Many people will boast about spending time doing something other than praying, as though praying is not *really* doing anything. However, prayer is the most profoundly earthshaking activity we can engage in. We need to learn to become comfortable and eager to burn hours in His presence. We invest time in it, just like we do in learning and experiencing any other thing.

Being in a season of tarrying or waiting is not an excuse to bide time with tasks or activities to keep us busy. It isn't the time to fill ourselves with things of the world. Instead, we must fill that time interacting with the Lord. The time you would've spent serving the church or a ministry, fill with being with Him. Then, when He says to go, go! After that, come back and wait with Him once more. Your jobs or assignments will flow from being with Him.

ASSIGNMENT FLOWS FROM IDENTITY

God first made Adam in His image as a son. Then, He gave him a job. We often make even our work for God a greater identity than being His children. Many of us can become so busy doing things God has not asked us to do in the first place. If we are constantly laboring, we can't hear Him when He does ask us to do something.

God's foremost desire is to conform us into the image of His Son. When I am rooted deeply in my assignment as a son, I can be like Jesus.

> *Jesus said to them, "Truly, truly, I say to you, the Son can do nothing of his own accord, but only what he sees the Father doing. For*

> *whatever the Father does, that the Son does likewise." John 5:19 ESV*

When I am like Jesus, secure in my identity as a child of God, I only do what I see my Father do. I only say what I hear the Father say. When you approach life from this place of peace—*kathizo*—He can give you assignments.

When Adam sinned, his relationship with God was altered, but so was His assignment. Partnering with God to care for the earth was turned into toiling. Is this how ministry has become for you? Toiling and cursing the ground, trying to force it to bear fruit? Or are you a co-laborer with Christ?

> *And God raised us up with Christ and seated us with him in the heavenly realms in Christ Jesus. Ephesians 2:6*

Kings are seated as they exercise their power. This denotes being at peace and in control, functioning from authority. This is not to say that all assignments will be easy. Following Jesus can be hard, but as you learn to do it out of sonship, partnering with the Lord, you find joy, even in the middle of adversity and personal cost. It's sacrificial, yes, but it is not striving. God wants us to sit in authority with Jesus.

ASSIGNMENT FLOWS FROM RELATIONSHIP

"Peter, do you love me?"

"Yes."

"Then, feed my sheep."

Three times Jesus asked this.[88]

What we do for Him must flow from our love for Him. If it doesn't, our service is misplaced. We can't fake this. He knows our heart as He knows all things. The greatest commandment is to love God with all that we are. Then, the second is easier. When we love God, we will love others and serve others as He did.

But first things first.

Remember the Macedonians. They gave themselves fully and first to the Lord. When they did this, He gave them as a gift to others and used them greatly. Their sacrificial service became an example to inspire others.[89]

Let's not get the cart before the horse. If the "cart" is our service and works, then the horse that pulls the cart is a heart fixed on love for Jesus and nothing else. Only then is His burden light, even when it is costly.[90] When we are not motivated by our love for Jesus, the smallest of spiritual things can be heavy to us. We are behind the "cart" trying to push it forward. It's an impossible task that we will ultimately give up on. Even if we do not quit church, our hearts quit Him.

Love Him. Seek Him. Get close to Him. Then, He will place you in the body as He sees fit. And when the Lord places you, you don't have to grab, push, and demand your rights or make your own way. "A man's gift makes room for him and brings him before the great" (Proverbs 18:16). Let the gift He gave you make room for *you*. You don't have to make room for it. There will be no need to keep score or feel sorry for yourself when others receive ministry opportunities.

In John 21, Peter questioned what Jesus was going to do with John. Jesus responded, "What is it to you what I do with him? I asked you to follow" (v. 22). Don't fixate on how the Lord is using others and their assignments. You must simply focus on following Him, focus on your assignment. Rest in Him. Submit to Him. Follow Him. Allow Him to place you as He sees fit. And when He does, don't reject or resist it. Just do what He asks.

The hardest thing to realize is that it is really not about us. It must be about Jesus. His Kingdom. His strategy. What He needs from us at any moment. If He wants us on the frontline or in the background. In front of a room or face down in prayer in the back. Serving in the street, or away in the prayer closet. It is all about Him, His Kingdom, His glory.

It's all about Jesus.

ASSIGNMENT FLOWS FROM TRUST

As a disciple of Jesus, we must learn to say, as He did, "I will only do what I see the Father doing." What does the Father want? That's what I will do. We often keep ourselves very busy with good things that God did not necessarily tell us to do. Don't confuse good with God. Just because an activity is good doesn't mean it's what God is asking of *you* in that moment.[91]

How do we know the will of God? Scripture teaches us the general will of God. Prayer reveals His specific will for our lives. For example, the apostles knew from the words of Jesus that they were to go into all the world and make disciples. But God gave them specific directions through prayer and prophetic dreams which cities they should go to and which to avoid.[92]

You will bear more fruit in ministry when you learn to hear His voice, trust Him, and do what He says. You can build a great house, but if you don't slow down to ask what He wants, you will be laboring with no purpose. [93]

It has been said that Jesus would spend six hours in prayer, then two minutes on a demon. We spend two minutes in prayer, then wonder why we must spend six hours on a demon! Or, the early church prayed for ten days, preached for ten minutes, and saw thousands saved. We pray for ten minutes and preach for ten days, then wonder why we don't see revival. We must slow down, Hear Him, and simply obey what He asks of us. You can learn this now or spend many years and relearn it—the hard way.

A man who had sold all of his possessions and moved to Calcutta to work with Mother Teresa was once asked how he was doing. He replied, "I need clarity." To which mother Teresa replied, "You don't need clarity, you need to trust!" Think about it. Insistence on clarity constitutes a need to know the details out of fear you will not make the right decision. Trust is about reliance on God. Clarity says, *I am walking through the valley of the shadow of death; if someone doesn't turn the lights on, I'm going to die or freak out*. Trust says, *Though I walk through the valley of the shadow of death, I will fear no evil, for you are with me*.[94] Trust admits that you cannot see the danger that lies around every bend. That one slip could plunge you to death. Financial uncertainty. Sickness.

Fear. Betrayal. Grief. But trust knows in the worst of times, you have but one question to answer: "Is the Shepherd near me?"

Do I sense Him? Do I feel His breath? Do I hear His whisper?

If so, I pause when He says pause. I step when He says step. I go when He says go. I trust my Shepherd. Even if my heart is violently beating, my knees are weak, and all my sensibilities scream, *Run!* I trust my Shepherd. After all, He successfully navigated the valley of death before and came through to the other side, holding the keys to death, hell, and the grave. He knows the way through. He is the way, the truth, and the life.

This type of trust will develop in you as you make Jesus the center of your service and ministry.

Jesus Revival

Chapter Eleven
Jesus-Centered Leadership

> *All the elders of Israel gathered together and came to Samuel at Ramah. They said to him, "You are old, and your sons do not follow your ways; now appoint a king to lead us, such as all the other nations have."*
> 1 Samuel 8:4-5

Israel was kingless, but they were not leaderless.

At first, God was their King, and His word was their law. Then, as needed, He sent judges, prophets, priests, warriors, and commanders to serve the nation. These were all powerful leaders—Moses, Joshua, Deborah, Gideon, Samuel—but none of them were kings. Israel wanted a king. Notice what God told the priest-prophet Samuel when they demanded one.

> *Listen to all that the people are saying to you; it is not you they have rejected, but they have*

> *rejected me as their king. As they have done from the day I brought them up out of Egypt until this day, forsaking me and serving other gods, so they are doing to you.*
> 1 Samuel 8:7-8

God then warned them through Samuel of all the harm a king would bring them. The people refused to listen to Samuel. 'No!' they said. 'We want a king over us. Then we will be like all the other nations, with a king to lead us and to go out before us and fight our battles.' (1 Samuel 8:19-20). The real issue became apparent—the king was an idol. The king was a replacement for God.

Years before, after separating them from the other nations on Earth and giving them His law to guide and protect them, God promised that He would go before them in battle. "It is the LORD who goes before you. He will be with you; he will not leave you or forsake you. Do not fear or be dismayed" (Deuteronomy 31:8).

But Israel wanted a physical king to do this instead. They wanted a physical replacement of God's leadership in their lives. This showed a lack of trust and faith in a sovereign God, in asking for a human who could be controlled, manipulated, and replaced.

Kings look powerful, demand respect, and ride in chariots surrounded by a royal guard. They command attention. In other words, the image of a king makes people feel secure and gives them a false sense of assurance.

The truth is that a king—a superhero warrior—is just an illusion. It's a myth. Battles are fought and won by people and armies, not by individuals. Sometimes powerful warriors can be a catalyst for freedom, like when David slayed Goliath. However, the *people* must possess the land. If they don't, opposing armies will quickly destroy the breakthrough that the catalytic warrior initiated and overtake them.[95]

God warned the Israelites that they would not have a king to fight *their* battles, but they would fight the *king's* battles. People have an illusion that a king fights and wins battles, but rest assured, if a king is doing it, he's doing it on the backs of his people.

> *Samuel spoke all the words of the LORD to the people who were asking him for a king. He said, "This will be the manner of the king who will reign over you:*
>
> *He will take your sons and appoint them to his own chariots and horses, to run in front of his chariots.*
>
> *He will appoint some for himself as commanders of thousands and of fifties, and others to plow his ground, to reap his harvest, to make his weapons of war, and to equip his chariots.*
>
> *And he will take your daughters to be perfumers, cooks, and bakers.*

> *He will take the best of your fields and vineyards and olive groves and give them to his servants.*
>
> *He will take a tenth of your grain and grape harvest and give it to his officials and servants. And he will take your menservants and maidservants and your best cattle and donkeys and put them to his own use.*
>
> *He will take a tenth of your flocks, and you yourselves will become his slaves. When that day comes, you will beg for relief from the king you have chosen, but the LORD will not answer you on that day." 1 Samuel 8:10-18 ESV*

A leader guards, protects, and directs people so they can live well as the people of God, doing the works of God. A king, on the other hand, demands that people protect him. A leader serves and helps people, but people serve and help a king with *his* agenda. Battles will be fought, but they will be fought for vastly different purposes. A king will fight to build his kingdom, not guard the inheritances and promises of his people.

OUR KING—JESUS

Jesus came to reestablish the Kingdom of Heaven—the rule and will of God on Earth. The first Christians knew Jesus as their King. They clearly understood that there were two kingdoms at play in this world. And they had a decision to make: be part of the kingdom of Caesar or the Kingdom of Jesus. "These men [Paul and Silas] who have caused trouble all over the world have now come here . . . They are . . . defying Caesar's decrees, saying that there is another king, one called Jesus" (Acts 17:6-7).

When Jesus is truly at the center of our lives and churches, we will return to His ultimate leadership as our Lord and King. Since He is God in flesh, this is His rightful place, one that belongs to no other person—whether in title or function.

> *Now when Jesus came into the district of Caesarea Philippi, he asked his disciples, "Who do people say that the Son of Man is?"*
>
> *And they said, "Some say John the Baptist, others say Elijah, and others Jeremiah or one of the prophets."*
>
> *He said to them, "But who do you say that I am?"*
>
> *Simon Peter replied, "You are the Christ, the Son of the living God." And Jesus answered him, "Blessed are you . . . For flesh and blood has not revealed this to you, but my Father who is in heaven. And I tell you, you are Peter, and on this rock I will build my church, and the gates of hell shall not prevail against it."*
> *Matthew 16:13-18 ESV*

The original Greek word for church is *ecclesia*. An ecclesia in the context that Jesus was using was not a religious service or gathering. Rather, it was a governing assembly of citizens that ensured the will of Caesar—their king and god—was carried out in a city or territory. Any citizen of Rome had permission to be part of the ecclesia of Caesar in their city.

Notice that Jesus was establishing His Ecclesia based on an understanding of who He was. **"You are the Christ, the Son of the living God."** Considering this, we must broaden our understanding of Church—Ecclesia. It is more than a pastor and congregation that meets weekly in a building called a church, for the purpose of music, teaching, and preaching. Every believer, every citizen of Jesus' Kingdom, has a responsibility to ensure that the will and purposes of our King are fleshed out in their city.

> *[After Constantine legalized Christianity and encouraged the Christians to build buildings,] church soon moved toward sacred priests doing sacred rites at a sacred place on a sacred day. Unfortunately today, in many people's minds, "church" still means a building. Christianity has become part of their religious sacred life on Sunday, not their secular life the other six days.*[96]

Some will broaden the definition of *church* to say that it is not a building, it is people. That's partially true. It's people who do what? It's people—citizens of the Kingdom of Heaven—who do the will of their King. The purpose of the secular ecclesia was not for every citizen to do what he or she desired in the name of Caesar, or for them to impose their will on others in the name of Caesar. It was established as an assembly of citizens who would ensure that their king's vision for the community would be fulfilled.

FALSE KINGS IN THE CHURCH

In the church today, we often we see the people of God serving the personal ambition of a handful of leaders, rather than leaders empowering the people of God to do the will of their King. And too often the church is willing to sit by and expect a handful of "superhero warriors" to do the work of ministry for them. As we learned with the nation of Israel, this is impossible, and to desire it from church leaders is spiritual idolatry. We need Godly leaders in our lives, but their role is never to be king. Our King is Jesus.

The Ecclesia of Jesus is not just a weekly meeting with worship and a message. It is people who follow Jesus as His disciples, becoming a Kingdom of priests, ruling with the authority of Jesus under the power of the Holy Spirit, doing works of the ministry, and building up the spiritual family.

This means that every disciple of Jesus should be equipped and expected to do these things:

- Skillfully study the Bible.
- Share the Gospel and give answers about their beliefs.
- Pray, discern the voice of God, and prophesy with accuracy.
- Pray for the sick with healing, signs, and wonders following.

These activities are often reserved for church leaders. But according to Scripture and the practice of the early Church, these should be normative for all believers.

Jesus' Ecclesia has the authority to fulfill His will in a city. God has given the Ecclesia keys and authority to bind and loose. In other words, we must all win battles, occupy land, build houses, plant gardens, and raise families. We can't just wait for a pastor/king to do it for us.

The leaders of the church are there to serve, protect, guard, and train the people of God. But the people must do the work. Battles are rarely won without a general, but generals cannot win battles alone. Victory happens when armies are equipped and effective; the people must fight. Then they must learn to occupy and live in their land.

SUBMISSION TO GODLY LEADERS

God has given members of the Church leaders to oversee them. To operate in authority, we must understand and submit to their authority. Notice the attitude of the Roman Centurion who asked Jesus to heal His servant: "The centurion replied, 'Lord, I do not deserve to have you come under my roof. But just say the word, and my servant will be healed. For I myself am a man under authority, with soldiers under me' " (Matthew 8:9). His understanding of authority released a level of faith in Him that amazed Jesus and caused Him to say: "Truly I tell you, I have not found anyone in Israel with such great faith" (Matthew 8:10).

> *Have confidence in your leaders and submit to their authority, because they keep watch over you as those who must give an account. Do this so that their work will be a joy, not a burden, for that would be of no benefit to you.*
> *Hebrews 13:17*

What is the leadership that Jesus has established in His Ecclesia?

> *Christ himself gave the apostles, the prophets, the evangelists, the pastors [shepherds] and teachers, to equip his people for works of service, so that the body of Christ may be built up. Ephesians 4:11-12*

These five leadership functions in the church are often referred to as the five-fold ministry. If Jesus is the center of His Church, then the Church will honor the five-fold ministry as their leadership. Scripture also gives clear commands to the five-fold ministers—the elders of the church.

> *So I exhort the elders among you . . . shepherd the flock of God that is among you, exercising oversight, not under compulsion, but willingly, as God would have you; not for shameful gain, but eagerly; not domineering over those in your charge, but being examples to the flock. . . . Likewise, you who are younger, be subject to the elders. Clothe yourselves, all of you, with humility toward one another, for "God opposes the proud but gives grace to the humble."*
> *1 Peter 5:1-3, 5*

While leaders guide, direct, strategize, and care for us with authority, they are not kings. They are directing, equipping, and preparing the Ecclesia to build Jesus' Kingdom. So we must align with their vision and oversight.

- Allow the apostles to align and realign the Church to a proper foundation and strategy (comparable to the Old Testament generals and commanders).
- Allow the prophets to give direction and correction (comparable to the Old Testament prophets).
- Allow the evangelists to lead the charge and help break through community and regional strongholds (comparable to the Old Testament warriors).
- Allow the shepherds to guard and care for the Church family (comparable to the Old Testament judges).
- Allow the teachers to teach the ways of God (comparable to the Old Testament priests).

It is time for the bride of Jesus to return to her fascination with her Bridegroom. Church leaders must stand as wedding attendants. To attempt to lure the attention of the bride onto us is idolatry and spiritual adultery. We are here to serve the needs of the bride and the Bridegroom. May the Church return to her first love—Jesus.

Chapter Twelve
Jesus-Centered Alliances

An alliance is a group of individuals or organizations that have joined together under a common goal. Often, the members of an alliance are not homogenous— they are of different backgrounds, beliefs, and ways of life. Think of an alliance of nations or businesses. While being incredibly distinct and separate, with their own ways of operating, they can unite to accomplish something they couldn't do on their own.

With Jesus at the center, church is about more than a local congregation, denomination, or theological tradition. You desire to see Jesus lifted up across your region, county, or city because, after all, church is about Him, not your local congregation. And for that matter, it's not about the congregation across the street either. The need to align with other churches who have a heart for the exaltation of Christ is extremely important. To have a lasting and profound Kingdom impact, churches must learn to rally together with Jesus as their common mission.

THE CHURCH OF THE REGION

The New Testament church functioned and structured itself differently than the churches most are familiar with. Church congregations were often families which met in households, guided and directed by elders who were more mature in the faith. Sometimes there would be hundreds or thousands of these small congregations across a city or region. When the Holy Spirit would address these believers, He was not talking to a single congregation, but to the Church of the region.

Each congregation saw itself as a part of the body of Christ operating in their area. While distinct, there was a common thread woven into their community which united every small church with every other church in their region. This is similar to the way in which many tribes and clans have historically functioned—a group of families and smaller tribes that, while spread across a territory, saw themselves as part of the same nation of tribes.

What would the Holy Spirit have to say about the unity of the churches in your region?

OBSTACLES TO FORMING ALLIANCES

Competition. There is an abundance of animosity among ministries that manifests in divisiveness. Competitiveness between ministries is based in selfish ambition, pride, and jealousy. Many church leaders are focused on building their own personal empires under the guise of building Christ's Kingdom. This breeds defensiveness and territorialism. Empire building in the Kingdom disables the possibility of unity between ministries.

We must all actively resist division within the body of Christ. We should not rejoice in someone leaving their church to run to ours. When people have issues with another ministry that we should see as our ally in faith, are we secretly glad to see that ministry weakened, or do we ask them to sit down and work out differences with their old churches before accepting them into our membership?

Many church leaders become intimidated by other churches' success, growth, and impact, while simultaneously, other leaders try to swallow up smaller congregations by stripping and looting them of members, so they can become the "superior" ministry. These attitudes drive many to see other ministries as their enemies and undermine a unified Church in a region.

We must stop seeing other churches as competition. We are often too eager to believe bad about those who, in the end, share the same mission: the glorification of Jesus. While churches waste time competing for members, trying to outdo one another in presentation, and spreading disdain and divisiveness, the mission of Jesus is lost and pushed aside.

We become ineffective when we could achieve it in greater measure by our unity.

Scarcity of resources. Many churches are hard-pressed for resources, whether in the form of money or people. Too often they see themselves as righteous beggars in a crowd, trying to give the best sales pitch to those who might be able to provide them with more resources. Churches who view themselves as isolated and solitary institutions divide the resources in a community, leaving few with enough to function and grow.

This may be very controversial, but if the Church truly is about the exaltation of Jesus, the need for multiple venues to promote leaders to visible leadership positions is unimportant. The truth is that churches would often be better served by combining efforts with other churches, rather than maintaining separate buildings, leadership teams, staffs, and budgets. Sharing resources expands the abilities of a group. What one can do with some is no match for what many can do with much.

> *All the believers were one in heart and mind. No one claimed that any of their possessions was their own, but they shared everything they had. Acts 4:32*

I know of a town where multiple churches came together to host a weekly youth group as a neutral space for teenagers to grow and connect. They understood that unity amongst believers in their local high school was more important than a single church having a superior or more successful youth group.

What would it mean for churches to stop claiming that what God gave them was "theirs?" What would it mean if churches saw every blessing from the Lord as belonging to the Kingdom for its corporate purpose?

Lack of trust and care. The truth is, many pastors and church leadership teams do not trust other pastors or leadership teams in their community. They see each other as competition.

Doug Abner, a leader in the 2004-2006 revival in Manchester, Kentucky, shared that the key to the revival in their community was dozens of pastors who came together and learned to be friends. They would meet every Saturday morning for breakfast and prayer, and over the course of months, they began to truly care for each other. If one of them had been hurt, the others prayed for him. If one of them had been wounded by their church members, the others cared for him. He states:

> *We began to be protective over each other because we were friends. People were no longer able to pit pastors against each other because we cared for each other.*

On a rainy day in May, thousands of people gathered to pray for their community, and sixty-seven pastors stood in front of them and repented for having cared more about their individual congregations than they did about the city, Jesus, or each other. The Holy Spirit hovered over this community, and then miraculous, Godly change occurred in a short time. The details of this revival can be found in the docudrama, *An Appalachian Dawn*.

Control Issues. When churches attempt to unify and work together, there are often leaders who want to own or manage what the Lord is doing by taking more control or credit than they have been assigned. Even within Jesus-centered alliances, territorialism can find its way in through the insecurities of the leaders involved.

This is often caused by a lack of maturity. As children, we get possessive over simple things—toys, food, or roles while playing. We do not understand that others have personal desires and responsibilities that are separate from ours, yet can coexist with ours. Children are often jealous and unable to interact well with other children because, from the time they are born, they are reliant on others and fear that their care may be taken away. But eventually, children mature and not only peacefully coexist with others, but even sacrifice their own comfort to care for them (1 Corinthians 13:11, 1 John 2:13-14).

In organizations where one person holds a majority or all of the power, he or she may not function well with other leaders. They may not want to partner with others, but exercise control to feel more secure in their own abilities, build up their own list of accomplishments, or collect trophies. Many church leaders will try to beat others to the punch instead of going after the mission field in unity. The mindset should not be, "Let's do it first, so others can't." Instead, it should be, "Let's do it together so we can have the maximum impact for Jesus."

The inability to share power reflects a lack of respect for the responsibilities others have and a carelessness with the mandate of Jesus for church leaders. In a Jesus-centered church, ultimately, He is in charge. Other leaders are set below Him, stewarding His mission, which they undertake together. This is Jesus' Church, and we are just caretakers.

Embittered traditions. Are some beliefs and practices worth separating over? The simple answer is yes. However, the list of beliefs that we should be protective over and unwavering on is much smaller than the countless trivial arguments that cause church and denominational divisiveness.

Some beliefs are truly worth taking a hard stance on, such as salvation through Jesus alone and the authority of Scripture. But on nearly every other issue, we should be very quick to forgive and tolerate those with whom we disagree. If our mission and core beliefs are the same, we should make it a priority not to argue and divide ourselves over nonessential matters.

We will, of course, prefer to be around those who agree with us. There is a level of comfort that comes from associating with those who believe similarly to us. The problem comes when our own practices prevent us from working or even associating with Christians who think differently on secondary, non-fundamental doctrine.

Can we agree to come together to pray and seek God's face, that revival would come to the world around us? That lost souls would be saved from hell? That glimpses of heaven could come to earth through Jesus' Church?

Great believers throughout Christian history have come to different conclusions on secondary issues and still had great Kingdom influence. Arminianism vs. Calvinism. Spiritual gifts vs. Cessationism. The nuances of how the Trinity is one. Even if we feel others are wrong with their conclusions, they are likely seeking scriptural understanding on such things, and therefore we should extend them grace.

We should seek to settle disagreements and come to Scriptural consensus in our distinct, local church communities as we wrestle to understand Scripture. But then understand that we can flatly disagree with each other about other matters, but if we agree on the Gospel, then we make Jesus our Lord. If we agree that salvation is found through Him, we can unite to fulfill His mission together. We must see beyond our church, brand, or denomination. There are times to set aside our preferences to focus on the common good.

What enables us to do this? A crystal-clear focus on Jesus. When He is not at the center of our churches, we are stripped of our ability to function together.

It is easy to believe that our personal way of doing something is the best or only valid way of doing it. But we can be incredibly narrow-minded in our methods to the point of being unable to exist with those who operate differently from us.

What matters have Christians differed on in interpretation and practice for centuries? Could we be open to learning more in these areas? Could we make allowances for our differences because of our love for Christ? Rather than dismissing a practice or method that is foreign to us, could we seek to learn more about it and from it? In what ways does it fulfill Scripture? In what ways does it disobey Scripture? Does it make you uncomfortable? Why?

Acknowledge you could be wrong, and others could be right. Acknowledge you could both be wrong, or in different ways, you could both be right. Be the best Christian you can be and seek awakening in your church or denomination. If He leads you to understand more truth, follow Him. If He leads you away from your church or denomination, then follow. If He tells you to stay, follow. If others tell you to leave, follow Him!

THE STRENGTH OF ALLIANCES

Ministry team alliances. In the coming days, we must see the value of aligning and ministering alongside other strong ministries. If we are always the strongest and most gifted in the room, we should seek out new rooms. There is great power when strong ministries work together in the same harvest field.

For example, lone shepherds in a city or region could come together to form one local body with a powerful leadership team of multiple shepherds, aligned with the governance model of the first church. It could also look like itinerant prophets and evangelists conducting revival services or working together in cities. Too many people want their "fifteen minutes of fame," when Jesus desires to build dream teams who can achieve accelerated results by working together and pooling resources.

Regional church alliances. When under the harsh realities of persecution, it is important to have strong relationships with churches near you or in your region. These could be more beneficial than relationships with churches of your denomination far from you. The point is, strong networks need to form within denominations and across denominational borders. We must embrace what God is doing in our city, county, region, and state. When persecution comes, many of us may very well be ostracized from our churches and denominations, so we must learn to work together.

I am not promoting the abandoning of denominations. I am encouraging you to see how the Kingdom of God is at work immediately around you. There might be active five-fold ministry around you that is highly in tune with what God is speaking to your local city, county, or region.

I believe God is calling us to see things from a regional perspective. We will not all be good at everything. What if we had regional revivals that moved from church to church, county to county? What if we were able to identify the true God-called evangelists that He is placing in our region? What if we could listen to the prophets that would warn us of the dangers in our region? What if we could understand apostolic blueprints that might look different than what our denomination is doing state or nationwide, but would look like what God is doing in our region?

What if we did not all decide to run back to our churches and attempt to be the one that does this first? Be the one that owns it or controls it? Instead, can we recognize what God is doing right now, as we gather and understand that He is forging a new path forward—that we need each other?

SUGGESTED WAYS TO ALIGN

Corporate prayer gatherings. Our relationship with God has been so individualized that we are void of the power that only comes through praying with others. This includes not just uniting with believers from your church congregation, but also with other churches for corporate prayer.

We do not have to agree on everything to pray together. We can even think our brother or sister is wrong about some theological issues, but if we agree on the Lordship of Jesus, we can pray together with grace and tolerance for each other.

Coordinated prayer strategies. Often in a city or community, multiple churches will come together to maintain a consistent, if not 24/7, center for prayer. This comes from a common goal to have a place for constant prayer in our cities. Coordinating people from multiple groups to pray yields a much larger, and therefore more effective, pool of intercessors and worshipers.

It's often hard for a single church to maintain a consistent and continual prayer covering over their region. However, if multiple churches join together and contribute, the work can be managed easier with greater results.

Region-wide evangelism events. Hosting events to reach the lost is more effective when multiple ministries partner together. By coordinating efforts, resources, teams, and areas of influence, we can maximize our collective work.

This has historically been the strategy of the Billy Graham Association. They would reach out and bring together sometimes hundreds of churches of many backgrounds to unite under the mission of Jesus. If everyone worked together to bring the Gospel to an area, the resulting impact would be greater than what any church could have done alone.

Region-wide humanitarian relief. A single church can only maintain so many ministries; it has a finite capacity for community impact. Several churches working together can maintain a homeless shelter, a recovery and rehabilitation center, or a food pantry. These are all visions that we should agree are necessary. They would be easier if we accomplished them as a team instead of as competing individuals.

What Kingdom solutions can we bring to our communities when we work together? How could our alliances put Jesus back into the central place of our region?

Jesus Revival

SECTION III
THE WAY FORWARD

Chapter Thirteen
Church as Usual is Over

Many traditionally minded churches are praying fervently for revival, but if a church is truly awake, they will expect to receive a harvest, and they will experience one. Churches operating as usual, though, will not be able to handle the load of a harvest.

I often ask church leaders this question: "If God sent revival to your church this weekend, would you know what to do with the harvest?" Or, more specifically, "If one hundred new people were saved this week in your church, what would you do with them?" Hint: just telling them to come back to church next week is not enough.

MINDSETS TO OVERCOME

The status-quo church calendar. Pleasant Bible studies and self-improvement sermons will not be enough. Routine

Sunday school lessons, Vacation Bible School, choir practice, and spring and fall revivals will not contain the harvest. These activities might build church attendance but will do little to prevail against the onslaught of the winter of persecution that faces the church.

There's nothing inherently wrong with these things, but even as different seasons require different clothes, new wine requires new wineskins.

One of the primary obstacles to revival is the lack of spiritual fervency in the church to both be and make disciples of Jesus. We are complacent and largely idle, but harvest and winter seasons are quickly approaching. We must prepare. We do not have the luxury of being nominally committed or involved only when it's convenient. Jesus has called us into His mission, and we must respond.

Resistance to growth. Large church growth does not automatically equal heresy, and small church size does not automatically equal truth. We are praying and preparing for an awakening in the church and for the harvest that will follow. That means biblical churches can and will grow.

After all, the first church described in Acts was highly potent in the Holy Spirit, grew in number by three thousand in one day, and added people every day after that. Some of the largest churches in the world, with hundreds of thousands of members, preach a strict Gospel message. Their secret lies in their prayer life, their ability to connect with the culture around them, and their intentional effort to empower every disciple to make and care for new disciples.

Preaching a true Gospel is not the primary reason many churches remain small. Instead, their loss of spiritual fervency for prayer is to blame. Others are no longer connecting with the community around them, and far too many are not empowering every believer to make new disciples.

This is not to say every church growth tactic is good (more about that in the next chapter). Connecting with people effectively and speaking the Gospel understandably is imperative for churches to grow. But it begins with a mature church family that can disciple new believers in both word and deed.

Territorialism and uninvolved church members. Possessiveness and jealousy over the church and the roles of its members and leadership must end. We need many workers in the fields. We can't just fight to preserve our lone spot in the church. The uninvolvement of most church members while the pastor and a handful of deacons or other leaders assume all the responsibility must also end.

Churches of all sizes, large and small, traditional and contemporary, with paid staff or volunteers, will need to adjust to reap and accommodate the incoming harvest. When it's time, we must have all hands in the field. If we do not, the harvest will rot. Likewise, if we do not have structures in place to care for the harvest until it can fulfill its intended purposes, it will rot in harvest piles in the coming winter of the church. I've witnessed many revival seasons that ended with a great harvest, but the harvest was lost because the church did not know how to nurture it.

As a spiritual family, we must be prepared to care for spiritual babies, discipling them into mature and reproducing adults. We must equip and expect spiritual maturity in our churches. This means it's time to grow up, so we can help others grow up. It's time to get out of the highchair, so there is room at the table for new believers. And don't get me wrong, they don't get to sit there long, either. They, in turn, will grow to disciple others.

The days of "my church, my needs" and "coddle me, serve me" are over. If harvest is coming, the church does not have the luxury of being complacent, sitting on the sidelines with our schedules jam-packed with the priorities of the world. Let's not crave milk when we should be cooking for others. These infant desires in our churches must end:

- Receiving the benefit of a spiritual family without responsibility to that family
- Being blessed without blessing others
- Enjoying a quality, healthy church environment without contributing time or money to it
- Being carried through crisis, but having no availability to meet others' needs
- Receiving support and encouragement, but having no time to connect with the family of God
- Enjoying the security and protection of a church family, yet constantly rebelling against and tearing down spiritual leadership and direction
- Expecting that leaders "fix" members who have wrecked their own lives by active rebellion against and disobedience to truth

Faulty church and church-leader expectations. Many people are comfortable with primarily expressing their spirituality through routine or convenient church attendance. They hope to find or create a church that will keep their kids happy or their spouse interested. However, it will take more than entertaining services, youth groups, and Wednesday Bible clubs to reap and care for the harvest.

Many others simply do not realize that God has called them to involvement in the making of and caring for new disciples. They assume that is the job of preachers and church leaders.

The model of a pastor who alone preaches and cares for the flock, visits all the sick, leads everyone to the Lord, and does the primary work of the church cannot be found anywhere in the Bible or the early Church record. Neither can congregations with church members who solely sit and watch the activity of the church, feeling the pastor should thank for them for showing up on Sunday, along with a few who sing or teach Sunday School. Or those who claim to be saved, yet give no evidence of Christ's desires for the Word and prayer, growth, loving and serving others, sharing the Good News, using their resources for the Kingdom of God, and submitting themselves to the watch-care of local, Godly elders.

We must relearn what it truly means to be a Christian—a follower of Jesus.

REDISCOVERING THE RESPONSIBILITY TO MENTOR

Not every believer is a gifted Bible teacher or a five-fold minister. But nearly every believer is capable of mentoring another believer. Not only that, Jesus expects this of us.

Equipping the saints for service involves more than having people fill out spiritual gift questionnaires and plugging them into ministries to keep Sunday mornings going strong.

Paul was clear that our ministry is one of reconciliation. We preach the Gospel and bring men and women to a right relationship with God through Jesus. We make disciples and teach them to obey *everything* Jesus commanded.

> *All this is from God, who reconciled us to himself through Christ and gave us the ministry of reconciliation: that God was reconciling the world to himself in Christ, not counting people's sins against them. And he has committed to us the message of reconciliation. We are therefore Christ's ambassadors, as though God were making his appeal through us. We implore you on Christ's behalf: Be reconciled to God. 2 Corinthians 5:18-20*

When Paul says "we," He means *every* believer. The primary ministry of every believer is to reconcile the world to God through Christ.

Are there things that must be in place when the church gathers corporately? Of course, that's tending to family responsibility. Should the church engage and serve the needs of the poor and the community? Of course, that's loving your neighbor as you love yourself. Disciples of Jesus do both. But the disciple can never negate the command given to all of us to make and teach new disciples. This is the ministry of reconciliation.

If only strongly gifted teachers have the opportunity to disciple or lead people in church, a huge percentage of the church is discounted and we are failing in our calling to prepare the saints for ministry: "And he gave the apostles, the prophets, the evangelists, the shepherds and teachers, to equip the saints for the work of ministry, for building up the body of Christ" (Ephesians 4:11-12).

The works of service that Scripture commands church leaders to train the church to do is to preach the Gospel, accompanied by signs and wonders, and to make, baptize, and mentor new disciples. And Paul explicitly instructed older believers to mentor and teach new believers. Only in our Western mindset do we confuse teaching with standing in the front of a room of obedient students lined up in rows.

To mentor others effectively, you need the following:

- To have been mentored yourself and demonstrated growth.
- The oversight of a more mature believer.
- A good curriculum or study to serve as a track or guide.

Our churches are full of people who do not want the responsibility of mentoring other disciples. Sometimes it's insecurity. Sometimes fear. Sometimes lack of training, and sometimes, it's a lack of salvation.

It's unfair to expect someone to do something we have not trained them to do. We must prioritize teaching and equipping every believer. But understand, we are not called to create churches for people who just want to attend church services and wait to die and go to heaven. We are called to equip the saints for works of service.

If the "saints" do not want to be equipped for works of service, we cannot change our mandate from the Lord just to keep them around. The church equips them, the Holy Spirit empowers them, but we must also *expect them* to fulfill the Great Commission. When you do, you may be accused of being judgmental, uncaring, unloving, a bad pastor, and many other things. These are just the complaints of rebellious hearts that are not submitted to the commands of Scripture. They are ultimately rebellious against the Lord. You will not honor Him by caving to their demands.

If you are a pastor or leader and serve in this type of environment, don't immediately try to turn everything on its head. You need strategy and a plan. People need to be taught and then provided opportunities. But those who refuse to grow and be trained should not be allowed to dictate the course of the church or your actions. Begin with those who are teachable and stay faithfully obedient to the Lord.

Refer to Appendix II for some practical ways to begin implementing a mentor-based discipling system in your church.

Chapter Fourteen
Subtle Dangers in the Contemporary Church

I acknowledge that I wrote this chapter from my own personal experience in leading a congregation for over twenty years. However, multiple conversations with church leaders and extensive research have shown that many others have reached similar conclusions.

From the beginning of my ministry, I have had a heart to reach those who were far from God, particularly those who had rejected traditional church and discarded God in the process. As I prepared for pastoral leadership and even as a young pastor in the early 2000s, "seeker-sensitive" was not a dirty phrase to me. When you love Jesus and have a heart for people who are far from God, you desire to build bridges to connect them. Being seeker-sensitive simply meant that you were sensitive to the gaps that existed between the church and those who were spiritually seeking.

Among other things, it also meant approaching church gatherings with an awareness of the following:

- Spiritual seekers might not understand church language; use words they understand or define "churchy" words when used.
- Spiritual seekers might not know the Bible, so explain its stories.
- Spiritual seekers have questions about God, the Bible, and Jesus; try to answer them.
- Spiritual seekers probably will not have loyalty to styles of music that are hundreds of years old, so use current music to engage them.
- Many people are visual learners; use visual aids to support the spoken Word.

UTILIZING CREATIVE, RELEVANT METHODS IS SCRIPTURAL

The premise behind engaging the culture with the message of Jesus is not wrong. We must become all things to all men so that we might win some (1 Corinthians 9:22). Paul spoke to pagans about the "unknown God," even quoting their poets (Acts 17:16-34). Bridging the divide between culture and the church's message is not only necessary, but biblical. The revived church throughout history has a track record of doing this. What we now consider traditional was at one time new. Many things that are now sacred were at one time secular.

Hymn writers such as the great reformer Martin Luther were criticized for using popular melodies of the day to bridge the gap between doctrine and the populace. The revivalist D. L. Moody was criticized for using an organ in his evangelistic meetings. Even Sunday School classes were banned at one time in many U.S. churches.

Let's be clear: you can be a highly gifted communicator employing creativity in your preaching and still preach the truth. All creative communicators are not heretics. Dullness does not equal truth, and creativity does not equal heresy. Creativity is a gift from God and can be used to express worship to Him. Worship styles vary across the world from culture to culture and have varied throughout history.

God is the Creator, and He has instilled creativity in His children. One look at a sunset or a field of flowers is proof enough that God enjoys the use of creativity and vibrant color. Even the Hebrew Tabernacle—which God designed—was full of colored material which was difficult to make in that era. Hebrew worship employed instruments and energetic as well as contemplative times of worship.

A creative technician can use the backdrop of a worship environment as skillfully as an artist uses a canvas. Songwriters and musicians can create new expressions of worship to God with their words and their instruments. A person skilled in using social media and online tools can engage people with the church and its message. A pastor or communicator can employ props, multi-media, and graphics to help a highly visual society learn biblical truth. Jesus was a gifted storyteller who no doubt used the visuals of nature around him to illustrate biblical truth (e.g., "consider the lilies of the field, the birds of the air" in Matthew 6, and "A sower went out to sow his seed" in Luke 8).

Creatively connecting with culture is not inherently wrong, but we need to exercise caution in doing so.

SUBTLE DANGERS IN CULTURAL RELEVANCE

The focus can gradually fade away from Jesus. As you build a distinct church "brand," you end up inadvertently putting a great deal of emphasis on the sermon, the series, the creativity, the children's programs, and other things, which can subtly lead to less emphasis on Jesus. The danger that must be avoided in a highly creative church environment (as well as in other church environments) is the shift to make people the motivation behind our efforts, and not Jesus. We may be tempted to do more and more to keep people coming back.

As much as we may not want to admit it, people can become more attracted to our methods than our message. Creativity can overshadow the Word and create a buzz that keeps people interested. Rather than enhancing worship and learning, it can distract from Jesus. This does not mean we should discard creativity in church, we just need to keep it in proper perspective.

Traditional churches can face the same issues as well. One can appeal to traditions to keep people coming back and still shift away from Jesus. Tradition itself can become an idol.

The attempt to be relevant can change our message. There is also the danger of becoming so relevant to our society that it compromises our message. More than one church-planning team has balked at the idea of singing a song from a "charismatic" church, despite the song's scriptural validity. Others have rejected the notion of singing a hymn because of its "tradition," yet have no problem with singing and playing secular songs with lewd or questionable undertones during their services in order to "build a bridge" to the unbeliever.

It's true that secular music that speaks to pain or paints a picture of grace can be a bridge to an unbeliever, but relevance can be a slippery slope. It crashes at the point where methods interfere with and reshape the message itself.

The seeker-sensitive mantra that I learned was, "Create a safe place to share a dangerous message." The problem is that the message itself destroys the safe, comfortable atmosphere that we often attempt to create. In order to keep the atmosphere "safe," the message is often inadvertently altered. The heavier aspects of our message are overlooked, while the benefits of the Gospel are accentuated.

Not all unbelievers and visitors are searching for truth. As a matter of fact, many might even like you, your church, your groups, your friendship, your worship gatherings, or your sermons, but have little or no interest in following Christ. Not everyone who comes to church, claims salvation, and seeks to be involved truly loves Jesus. There is a long list of reasons that attracts believers and unbelievers to a church. When the teachings of Jesus are emphasized, these people often bail.

Many times, the danger is not in the preacher saying something wrong, although heresy and distortions of grace are filling the pulpits. The subtle danger is in the content we avoid preaching on. We avoid naming sins. We avoid the controversial claims of Christ. We avoid the demands of discipleship. A high number of people reject truth and desire preachers to scratch their itching ears, and far too many preachers are obliging.[97]

Jesus said, "Blessed are those who are not offended because of me" for a reason.[98]

We can attempt to shelter people from the Holy Spirit. We often shield people from the intense work of the Holy Spirit, whether that be a convicting call for repentance, a supernatural work through signs and wonders, or fervent prayer. We fear these things will "turn off" unbelievers who are spiritually seeking.

Remember, not everyone who comes is truly spiritually seeking. It's important to explain what's happening when the Spirit moves, to avoid confusion. But we cannot shield people from the very Power that would transform their lives. The apostles did not have a gradual way to introduce people to Him. Their first step was this: *preach the Gospel with a demonstration of the Holy Spirit's Power.* Even as on the day of Pentecost, when He comes, there will be polarizing reactions. Some will be perplexed, and some will be amazed. Some will mock, some will marvel.[99] (Note: this is not an excuse to be odd for the sake of seeming spiritual, but is an acknowledgement that the Holy Spirit's activity can at times seem odd.)

At best, we can create interest in people, but not hunger. Only being born again creates true spiritual hunger. Like a baby needs, craves, and demands nourishment, so a born-again spirit will desire the Word and presence of God. And people can only be born again by the transforming power of the Holy Spirit.

I've found that once the glory of God is in a congregation, true conviction, salvation, deliverance, signs, and wonders are normal. Gimmicky methods and preaching seem very shallow and awkward. It's like comparing plastic jewelry to a million-dollar necklace. It's fun to play with, but once you possess the real thing, there is no comparison.

Will we pray and contend until revival comes, or will we resort to tricks and gimmicks that appeal to the flesh and emotions to keep people engaged or attending?

Life-changing, relational discipleship can suffer for the sake of worship services. We spent years perfecting attractive, creative, entertaining, and engaging worship gatherings. I was proud of these services. I was proud of the fact that I preached straight-up, candid truth as well. But it did little to make disciples of Jesus. We attracted crowds and had a lot of engaging community ministries. Ten years in, we realized that this was doing very little to create disciples who lived and walked as Jesus did. Which, after all, is the Great Commission.

Jesus did not say fill buildings. He said to make disciples and teach them to live as He lived (Matthew 28:18-20).

The problem is that the church, as a whole, puts too much emphasis on the corporate worship service alone to effectively make disciples. I am not discrediting the role of preaching. God uses the foolishness of preaching to confound the wise and bring people to repentance.[100] But public preaching was not the only method Jesus and the apostles used to make disciples.

- Jesus preached and taught the crowds, but He mentored His disciples. He also built a community of believers with a larger group of seventy disciples that modeled and lived out His teaching together (Luke 8, 10).
- The early church met in the Temple courts and from house to house (Acts 2:42-47).
- In Scripture, older people were instructed to teach the younger. The inference here was life on life modeling and feedback (Titus 2:3-5).
- Paul mentored Timothy and other travelling companions and gave them the task of passing to others what he taught them (1 Timothy 1:2, 2:2).

Although we attempted to take people deeper spiritually through small groups, people who were coming for the "show," through usually indirect ways, kept the true spiritual fervency of our church low and shifted resources away from mentoring and discipling environments. This is not a problem only inherent in contemporary churches. Traditional churches are also full of people who come for the gatherings but have little interest in taking steps toward deeper discipleship.

Those who are passionate about the Lord end up expending a lot of energy engaging those who show up for reasons other than Jesus. There is usually pressure to keep the Sunday morning attendance high. This often happens at the cost of discipleship and relationships. Spiritually potent people are often drowned in the relentless need to keep church consumers satisfied, all in the name of reaching those who are spiritually seeking.

In a serving team model, people are quickly connected to Sunday serving teams to keep them connected to the church. This usually demands a lot of time throughout the week for rehearsals, lesson preparation, etc. When you ask people to attend a small group in addition to a team preparation time, they usually end up picking or choosing one or the other.

This is not always because people are insincere Christians. It is due to the demands of daily life. Non-traditional work schedules, single parenting, or both parents working outside the home puts an incredible strain on people's lives and schedules. The time for intentional focusing on mentoring and discipleship becomes less and less. Even when you try to turn part of the team rehearsal time into discipleship, the ministry task inadvertently takes over the meeting time or turns it into a several hour meeting that strains an already stretched schedule.

Character can easily be overlooked for the sake of talent. Manning the teams with gifted people can often become more important than the call of discipleship. Truthfully, we often do not dig too deeply into a talented person's personal life, because we'd rather not know if there is an unchecked pattern of sin. If we find one, we know we would either have to ignore, condone, or confront it. Confronting it, even in love and humility, can often lead to someone leaving rather than receiving correction and changing. Our avoidance, then, is often disguised under the mask of wanting to show love vs. judgement. Yet true love warns and restores the fallen. Love does not leave the sinful in bondage without offering freedom.

People can think they are saved because they enjoy our church. A popular idea in the church is that we should let the lost belong to our community before they believe. The general premise behind this is that we should befriend people, even if they do not yet believe in Jesus.

There is nothing wrong with that idea. Jesus was a friend of sinners. But great care must be taken to ensure we do not give people a false assurance of salvation. We cannot allow people to confuse friendship in church members or the enjoyment of church with having a relationship with Christ.

I am not suggesting that churches should be exclusive, elitist clubs that some are not good enough to join. Jesus preached and ministered to the crowds. But before they belonged to the company of disciples, they had to leave all they knew, love Him more than anything, pick up their cross, and follow Him. In other words, He had to be Lord of their lives.

A study of over 250,000 church attenders in churches of all sizes, styles, and denominations revealed that the longer a person is in church without deciding to follow Christ, the less likely they are to do so. They get lulled into a fake illusion that liking or being involved with the church somehow indicates they are okay with God.[101]

We can all probably give examples of someone who attended church for several years and then decided to serve Christ. That does happen. However, it is very dangerous to make one feel like they are part of the church without being a disciple of Jesus. Life change is normative for true believers. If you profess faith in Jesus, and you are truly born again, change will ensue. We must be careful in our attempts to be inclusive and bridge gaps to the world, so that we do not lower the demands of discipleship for those who call themselves Christian. This means that church discipline should be enacted to the point of removing a person from church fellowship if they refuse to confront and turn from gross patterns of sin.

What attracts people keeps people. At the church I pastored, in theory, we insisted that Sunday mornings were just a step to the larger discipleship picture, and they were. On paper and in meetings. The issue is, what attracts people keeps people. People often give a nominal commitment to the things that would help them grow most—discipleship, mentoring, and accountability relationships, and too often, church leaders give nominal resources to the areas as well.

Small groups and Sunday School classes do not automatically equal discipleship. They can play a role, but the critical aspect of relational mentoring in key areas of Godliness is often neglected in discipleship. Often small group and other church leaders are subtly discouraged from confronting people with difficult truth about sin and Christlikeness, particularly with people who are not committed to growth and quit attending a group or church because they are offended. And far too often, small group leaders and Sunday School teachers are appointed based primarily on willingness or giftedness, with an inadequate emphasis on spiritual maturity and character.

We had New Member Growth classes that taught the principles of discipleship, but did not provide the mentoring relationships necessary for true discipleship to transpire . The practice of Jesus, the apostles, and effective churches around the world shows that discipleship happens best in this context, where a mentor can give a new disciple access to their life as well as real-time feedback as they attempt to learn the ways of Jesus.

There is nothing wrong with preaching to crowds and filling buildings. The apostles did this, but *Why are they coming?* and *Why are they staying?* are questions any responsible church leader needs to ask.

We always had a desire for people to encounter the very real, living, life-transforming message of Jesus. We always envisioned that our core group would grow, and there would be even more people with spiritual fervency to make and care for new disciples.

The problem was, the system was too demanding, and it focused on corporate gatherings over relationships. It was inherently flawed. It attracted people who, for the most part, were interested in what they could get from God and not what they could give. Once we course-corrected and began to emphasize the cost of following Jesus, many left, but those who stayed grew and have become reproducing disciples of Jesus. The growth is slower. It takes time to relationally disciple. We have encountered problems with these new methods, but they are healthy.

Some questions for church leaders to consider: Are people coming to your church as transfers from other churches, ones who simply like your worship style and your service better? If so, you could just be attracting spiritual consumers, rather than making disciples of Jesus.

Are people coming because they want to grow deeper spiritually and know they can do that at your church? Are unbelievers getting saved and turning into spiritually fervent, committed, reproducing disciples of Jesus?

If not, it is possible that no matter how well-intentioned your efforts might be, you could be making disciples of your church's style and not of Jesus. And this is a painful truth to admit.

Chapter Fifteen
The Fire of a Revived Church

As we conclude this discovery of how to help the Church return to the fire and fervency of first love for Jesus, we must once again examine its core mission. When asked what the greatest commandment in the Law was, Jesus replied:

> "You shall love the Lord your God with all your heart, and with all your soul, and with all your mind." This is the great and foremost commandment. The second is like it, "You shall love your neighbor as yourself." On these two commandments depend the whole Law and the Prophets." Matthew 22:37-40 NASB

We call this the Great Commandment. When we examine the behavior of the early Church in the book of Acts and throughout the New Testament, we see that after Jesus returned to heaven, the disciples were red-hot with love for

God and loved their neighbors even as they loved themselves.

Now fast-forward sixty years later. Jesus was speaking a corrective message to the churches through the Apostle John, who was nearing his own death, exiled on an island: "I know your works. You have the reputation of being alive, but you are dead" (Revelation 3:1 ESV).

Author John Bevere points out that there must have been something that made this church look alive! After all, if a church has fifteen members who are disconnected from the world around them and miserable, who only half-heartedly go through the motions when they gather, it probably doesn't have a reputation for being alive. [102]

There are many churches that, on the surface, do look alive. They show many signs of life. They have energetic music, rooms full of enthusiastic people, vibrant children's programs, and impactful activities in the community. If these factors are present, it might be hard to think that a church is, in fact, dead.

How do you know if your church is alive, dead, or at best asleep? To answer this question, you must consider two defining factors: Who are the burning ones in your church? What are they burning for? If a church is alive or has a reputation for being alive, people are pouring an incredible amount of passion and energy into it. It's entirely possible to be fired up for a lot of good things in the name of "church," but are people burning for the right things?

As Jesus said to the church at Ephesus:

You have persevered and have endured hardships for my name, and have not grown weary.

Yet I hold this against you: You have forsaken the love you had at first. Consider how far you have fallen! Repent and do the things you did at first. Revelations 2:3-5

This has also been translated as, *"You don't love me or each other as you did at first!" (NLT).*[103] This is a call to return to the basics of the Great Commandment: love God and love people.

Any church that seeks to create anything less than a family of red-hot burning disciples of Jesus who are willing to set aside their lives for the cause of Christ cannot rightfully call themselves a church in a true, biblical sense. Regardless of how much of a difference they think they're making, they are failing in their true mission.

BURN FOR JESUS

Our *first* commandment is a passionate love for God. All other commandments flow from it.

If people only come to church to get their Sunday morning fill, they aren't burning for Jesus. If people just want to punch the church clock, live like hell, and be assured of heaven when they die, they aren't burning for Jesus.

Do they love God with all of their heart, soul, mind, and strength?

Are they obsessed with Jesus?

Are they truly blown away by the love and goodness of Jesus and constantly talking about it?

You know there is a problem when the only things people say about your church are, "We have a great kids' program." "We have a very active youth group." "We've got a great band." "You will really like our preacher."

Instead, people should be eager to truthfully say, "When our church gathers, you truly encounter Jesus. If you gather with us, you can encounter Him as well. I don't know the way you will encounter Him, but you will!"

There is nothing inherently wrong with having an engaging children's program, an active youth group, a lively worship band, and acts of community service. However, if that's your church's only focus, these have become idols, or will soon be. This mindset must be identified, confessed, and turned from. Healthy churches will have some or all of these things, but this does not mean the people in that church are red-hot disciples of Jesus.

Do they burn for Jesus, face-to-face, with no additions?

BURN FOR MORE THAN FOR AN EXPERIENCE WITH CHRIST

The early Church experienced true revival. At and after Pentecost, fire, drunkenness, and spiritual gifts exploded everywhere. There was an enormous surge in salvation and conversion. The result of that experience was a passionate desire to love and trust Jesus—to learn and obey what He desires. They continued steadfastly in devotion to the apostle's teaching.

After you recover from a deeply spiritual experience, are you ready to do what Jesus says? Are you ready to *do* what He wants? Go *wherever* He wants? Are you ready to forgive *that* person? Love *that* person? Serve *that* person?

If you don't actively seek and live out the teachings and will of Jesus, then by definition, you are not truly a *follower* of Jesus. You might be experiencing Him, but you are not following Him.

BURN IN INTERCESSION

Is it normal for the believers in your church to intercede, to pray for God to change their communities?

Like the persistent widow who daily asked the judge for justice until he conceded, we must do the same in our appeals to God.[104] Persistent prayer warriors, who unwaveringly petition God day and night, do so with hope in His promises. They've heard and seen what He has done in the past. If there's any chance He'll do it again, they will not let Him rest, petitioning Him with continuous prayer. But to many, this seems like a waste of time.

A woman sent me this message recently:

> *Over half of the students in our high school are using drugs or vaping marijuana, often at school.*

> Members of our church would like to help and make a difference, but we don't know what to do.

I replied:

> I would begin by calling regular corporate prayer several times a week.
>
> I would petition God to send true revival to your community. Drugs are the lesser problem. They are a symptom of the real problem, spiritual emptiness, which will lead to eternity in hell. Engaging with passionate, fervent prayer for as long as it takes for God to send spiritual awakening is the only real solution. It's not easy.
>
> And this will be criticized by most Christians as not doing "enough," but Scripture and church history show me this is the only lasting solution. Someone must stand in the gap.

She followed up with:

> We have prayer meeting every other Wednesday which I am leader of.

Again, I responded:

> Go into intense, fervent prayer several times a week until something changes. Most will say that's not necessary, however, nothing else has

> *worked up to now. Throughout history it's the only thing that has truly changed a community.*
>
> *Try to find other believers from other churches that will gather and pray with you as well. Have prayer points. But pray in the spirit as much as you can. Let moanings and groanings of the Spirit regularly fill your room (Romans 8:26-27). Something must happen.*
>
> *Let the Holy Spirit intercede for you. Pray for God to send revival and tarry until He shows you what He wants you to do and then fills you with power to do it.*

She said she would present my idea to her congregation. It was not met with much enthusiasm.

What about you? Will you lay yourself as a living sacrifice on the altar of intercession day in and day out? Will you be the one who will rebuild the wall of righteousness and stand in the gap until it is rebuilt? Will you be a watchmen on the wall, seeing in the Spirit, and through prayer and prophetic utterance to warn people of the danger ahead? Will you give God no rest until He remembers the promises He made?

Be careful with dismissing this by saying, "I'm not an intercessor. I have another calling in the church." This is not a Scriptural response.

Red-hot, passionate love for God is normal for *all* believers. A desire to commune and talk with Jesus is normal for *all* believers. The first church often met for the sole purpose of prayer. Intense intercession is normal for a revived, alive church.

Duncan Campbell describes how a praying remnant patiently waited for the Lord to respond to their cries on the Isle of Lewis:

> *According to the report given me by the minister of the parish you find men waiting through the night in confidence that God was about to manifest His power. You find two elderly sisters on their faces before the peat fire three nights a week pleading one promise, I say one promise: "I will pour water upon him that is thirsty, and floods upon the dry ground." A promise made, as they declared, by a covenant-keeping God who must ever be true to His covenant engagements.* [105]

Where are those lingering and pleading with desperation that God would save their family? That He would send His floods upon the dry ground?

Instead of an intense desire to pray and seek God's face and power, we often find people who are disgruntled at being asked to linger and pray for their friends and families. Or they're angry at pastors for having the audacity to preach against sin and potentially offend their friends and family.

Those who truly burn for Jesus reject the lukewarm attitude of feel-good Christianity. Instead, they cry out with fervency to petition God to fill them and their community with *His* power. These are the true Kingdom bringers. Like the first apostles, they've been with Jesus. They are equipped in the Word, and they desire Holy Spirit empowerment that enables them to build the Kingdom.

Where is the prayer life of the leaders and pastors? We should see evidence of profound and consistent tarrying in the Spirit in our church leaders. This will not only be evident in their teaching and personal life, it will be evident through the Holy Spirit power they exude. It should be dripping off of them because they have been marinating in the secret place.

We need those who are willing to cry out to God whether the congregation is there or not. We need worship leaders who will sing to an empty room and worship from the floor before they worry about leading from a stage.

BURN FOR GOD'S WORD

Where is the passion to live out the challenges of Christ every day?

Ironically, a church can look really alive and be very excited about their engaging, creative teaching series, yet make no effort to live the Word that is taught. Creative teaching experiences are not in and of themselves wrong, but are the hearers living the Word?

A person who is incredibly passionate about the Word of God will see it rightly. They will see where they lack and be broken over it. However, often in churches that seem alive but are, in fact, dead, some of the people most passionate about "the cause" have little respect for the Word of God. They don't read it. They don't live it. They easily dismiss it.

BURN WITH CONVICTION OVER PERSONAL SIN

Where are the people asking God to change and deliver them from *their* sin?

This doesn't just include sins like addiction or any of the others we highlight to divert attention from our own sin. It also includes gossip, division, racism, pride, idolatry, lust, sexual immorality—both homosexual and heterosexual—along with every other work of the flesh.

Where are the people lingering and praying and asking for deliverance, or tarrying for power to go out in the world and bring deliverance? Where are the people helping each other overcome sin, rather than making excuses for one another?

BURN WITH A DESIRE TO MAKE NEW DISCIPLES

The question is not, *Do they burn with a desire to get people to come to church?* Instead, it should be, *Do they burn with a desire to make new disciples of Jesus, because they are passionately in love with Him and understand that every person on earth is the reward of His suffering?*

He has earned the right for every person to know who He is.

True evangelism is more than just inviting the lost to a bring-a-friend worship service and coaxing them into saying a prayer in the hope that they will be saved. True evangelism is spiritual warfare for a person's soul. It is bringing a person to Jesus and allowing Him to save them. It is giving them an opportunity to see the breathtaking glory of God in the face of Jesus, which results in full devotion to Him.

It is vitally important that you are equipped and empowered with Holy Spirit fire and power before you begin to make new disciples.

Carnal, complacent Christians, looking for a good time in church and a get-out-of- hell-free card, produce other carnal, complacent Christians, looking for the same. While this might fill up seats in a building, it will do nothing to transform your community. It will not prepare people to get ready for that great and terrible day of the Lord's return.

Before we reach the lost and bring them to Christ, we must first know Christ and follow His teachings ourselves. We must first become good disciples. We must burn for the Lord, grow in His Word, and begin overcoming sin. This takes time. But we must be willing, even if it takes longer than we thought or is uncomfortable. This is not a journey of comfort. It's about personal transformation, spiritual empowerment, and making other disciples of Jesus.

The only way to get equipped and empowered is to submit, to offer yourself to the discipline of training, knowing the Word, and tarrying before the Lord. You might have to wait for power, no matter how long it takes. Then, and only then, will you be equipped and empowered to make disciples.

The first disciples and apostles were all closely *equipped* by Jesus for three and a half years, and on the day of Pentecost, they were *empowered* by the Holy Spirit. He was poured out on them by Jesus after years of teaching and many days of tarrying.

So many churches are comfortable with pews filled with complacent Christians who go through the motions rather than producing disciples, or filled with those who are only interested in being encouraged and having nice experiences instead of being passionately and obsessively in love with Jesus.

Thanks, but no thanks. A real church:

- Raises up an army, not attenders.
- Seeks family, not fans.
- Cultivates ministers, not consumers.

You can easily find a church with a lesser vision who might be quick to use you and your gifts to build their ministry, with little to no regard for your spiritual vitality.

But a Jesus-centered church loves Jesus, the world, and you too much to throw you out on the frontline unskilled, unequipped, and powerless. We need people who know how to burn before the Lord. People who know how to wait until they are endued with power from on High. Then, they will go make new disciples. This is the pattern of Scripture and Church history.

BURN WITH CHRIST'S LOVE FOR EACH OTHER

I mean real love. The church can't be just a nice place to go on Sunday morning; it's a family. It's an environment where you are legitimately happy to get together with other believers.

Notice the love that the early church had for each other:

They devoted themselves to the apostles' teaching and to fellowship, to the breaking of bread and to prayer. Everyone was filled with awe at the many wonders and signs performed by the apostles. All the believers were together and had everything in common. They sold property and possessions to give to anyone who had need. Every day they continued to meet together in the temple courts. They broke bread in their homes and ate together with glad and sincere hearts, praising God and enjoying the favor of all the people. And the Lord added to their number daily those who were being saved.
Acts 2:42-47

Whether you're in prayer, discussing the Word, or enjoying a meal, the church should constantly be growing and living as a family with a singular mission and a shared love. But if gossip, carnal chit-chat, or pity parties with others is all that excites you, you've missed the point.

BURN IN EVERYDAY LIFE AND LANGUAGE

What is the prevalent topic of your conversation with others? Sports, politics, hobbies, current events, or God forbid, gossip? When was the last time you began a conversation with, "I was reading the Bible today, and look what God spoke to me!" or "While I was praying, God told me . . ." or "I am so convicted over this sin in my life. The Holy Spirit loved me enough to reveal where I was falling short."

Do you think it's strange or normal to see people passionately devote themselves to worship and prayer? I know from experience that if you suggest that people should spend hours in prayer and devotion to the Lord, you are often pegged as a religious fanatic—by other Christians. But the first Church was excited to meet together in the Temple courts *every day*. If a church would act similarly today, it would most likely be labeled as a cult. Why would this seem cultic for Christians, but perfectly normal for sports coaches to ask or even demand daily devotion from your family? The question is, *What do you burn for?*

KEEPING THE FLAME HOT

Passionate communion with God is the center of our faith.

We bring new believers into an environment of passionate prayer, convicting preaching, and supportive love and mentoring as they are discipled. But for many churches, when visitors and newcomers show up, or when they get into a groove of worship and outreach, the fire of God leaves. This happens when the leaders and church body slowly drift away from the power and passion in their own prayer lives. The solution is an unrelenting and constant connection to the Father in prayer.

Making yourself a living sacrifice, day in and day out, can be daunting. It takes over your life. Hence, you are a *living* sacrifice. This is not always comfortable. In your own effort, it is impossible. There is a constant allure for normalcy and comfort. Sometimes comfortable leaders teach us things to keep us comfortable because they themselves want to remain comfortable. In doing so, notice that they don't necessarily say that they want to get rid of the fire. Instead, they find excuse after excuse to just turn it down a bit.

Not too hot, not too cold. Not too much, not too little. Just right. That, my friend, is the textbook definition of lukewarm. And it might be just right for us to be comfortable, and it might be just right for our family and friends who are interested in our church but "put off" by prayer and holiness. The only problem is that it makes God vomit. [106]

A church does not get closer to fulfilling God's purposes by bringing the temperature down to accommodate people who have no desire to burn for Jesus.

We must stop feeling good about ourselves for creating events that people are eager to attend, yet that bring no conviction. We must stop patting ourselves on the back because unbelievers like our church and, at the same time, are comfortable with their sins. We must stop congratulating ourselves on the number of baptisms we have, while few are laying their lives down in sacrificial service to Jesus.

Church attendance, baptisms, and volunteering at church ministry does not mean you are a sold-out disciple of Jesus Christ. It can mean you have a reputation of being alive and full of fire, but are really dead, burning for the wrong things.

May the church return to the fire and fervency of our first love—Jesus.

Chapter Sixteen
Preparing for the Future

Every week, the American Church spends billions of dollars, coordinates hundreds of millions of volunteer hours, and produces services that are attended by tens of millions of people. Yet, in my opinion, despite all of the money, energy, and man-hours logged, we are doing *precious little* to actually prepare the average person to meet the three greatest challenges in our lifetime:

1. A great harvest of souls.
2. Increasing and impending persecution.
3. The return of Jesus.

This is a real problem!

We need millions of disciples *today* that are strong in the faith and can reach and mentor new disciples. We do not just need volunteers that keep the cogs of the church "machine" turning. Sadly, most pastors and church leaders are satisfied if people show up, the service is pulled off with few glitches, and the bills are paid. We must wake up! He did not call us to just put together and host good church services. He called us to make and equip disciples, who can make and equip disciples (Matthew 28:18-20, Ephesians 4:11-12, 2 Corinthians 5:11-21).

Something has to change! If we start now, we will be running hard to catch up, even if Christ delays His return by fifty years. This involves far more than just preaching harder or telling people they need to grow up in the faith! All the solid nuts and bolts plans and Spirit-filled strategies are useless if you do not understand the urgency of the times.

For the church to thrive, especially during hard times, we must create strong disciples of Jesus who are not dependent on church leadership to keep going. We must have disciples who know what to do if they are temporarily disconnected from the church body.

This does not mean that the church has no need for leaders. It simply means that healthy leaders help people mature. If cut off from their church leaders, will our members be able to shepherd, care for, and disciple their families, or the people in their apartment building, their trailer park, or neighborhood? Will they be a source of stability and strength to those in turmoil when disaster or unrest strikes, or will they spiral out of control like everyone else? We must have those who can function and thrive, even during hard times, because they are growing to spiritual maturity *now*. Most Christians cannot even cope during good times; what will we do when the horsemen of winter come?[107] Disciples of Jesus should:

- Live free from the opinion of man.
- Identify and overcome their besetting sins.
- Discern the voice of the Lord in their daily life.
- Pray effectually and fervently.
- Pray for others and prophesy with accuracy.
- Have a firm grasp of the basic doctrines of the apostles.
- Explain the Gospel to an unbeliever.
- Comfortably receive and give biblical advice and correction.
- Build a small family of believers with their family and friends.
- Show others how to do the same.

If we aren't equipping people to do these things, what are we doing? We must stop with simply teaching and hoping for the best. We must move from "you should" and "why aren't we" to "practically, here's how to . . ." We must be strategic. We must provide a *practical path* and *real-life opportunities* for people to learn to reach and disciple others.

THE RETURN OF JESUS

Around forty days after Jesus was resurrected, He returned to heaven. The apostles and most historical evangelists were motivated to share the Gospel because they believed Jesus could return—at any time—to judge the earth, and people would be unwarned and lost at His return.

> *"Men of Galilee," they said, "why do you stand here looking into the sky? This same Jesus, who has been taken from you into heaven, will*

> *come back in the same way you have seen him go into heaven." Acts 1:11*
>
> *Look, I am coming soon! My reward is with me, and I will give to each person according to what they have done. Revelation 22:12*

This created an urgency within them to share the Gospel with as many as they could.

> *"Therefore let all the house of Israel know for certain that God has made Him both Lord and Christ—this Jesus whom you crucified. . . ." And with many other words he solemnly testified and kept on exhorting them, saying, "Be saved from this perverse generation!" Acts 2:36, 40 NASB*

Jesus told multiple parables that illustrated the need to be ready for His Second Coming. He urged us to watch and pray and stay ready. It caused the apostles and early disciples to tell the world of Jesus, even when it caused them great pain and persecution. (Read Matthew 24:29-25:51.)

When you read Jesus' teachings in Scripture and see the amount of time He spent telling people they should be prepared for His return, it's astounding. He poses the question, "Will I find faith when I return?" He wasn't wondering if people would emptily say a prayer ensuring they would go to heaven when they die. He wanted to know if we would be living faithful lives. Does our faith amount to something we just say we believe in, or is it evidenced by how we live our lives? By our works? He taught us that we must live watchful, spiritually vigilant, and fervent lives. Lives that are about our Father's business.

We must stay alert. We are to watch and pray, to occupy—be faithful to tending our spiritual responsibilities—until He returns.[108] Instead, as a church we are largely preoccupied with the things of the world. Asleep. Forgetting our master could return at any point in time. Jesus warns against this attitude repeatedly.

This is why we must pray and preach the message of revival, for the Church to be awakened from sleep and return to the prevailing Ecclesia that Jesus founded. Revived. Full of life. Full of power. Walking in authority. Preaching the Gospel. Signs and wonders following. Reverent fear and awe filling the church.

THE COMING HARVEST

A return to expecting true responsibility and spiritual growth in every believer is the bedrock key to the future of the church's readiness for harvest, one that will endure through the persecution of winter.

> *And Jesus came and said to them, "All authority in heaven and on earth has been given to me. Go therefore and make disciples of all nations, baptizing them in the name of the Father and of the Son and of the Holy Spirit, teaching them to observe all that I have commanded you. And behold, I am with you always, to the end of the age." Matthew 28:18-20*

Not every disciple is called to stand in front of rooms and teach groups, but every disciple can preach the Good News to someone, and every Christian can teach a new believer how to follow Jesus.

> *But you will receive power when the Holy Spirit has come upon you, and you will be my witnesses in Jerusalem and in all Judea and Samaria, and to the end of the earth. Acts 1:8 ESV*

> *And there arose on that day a great persecution against the church in Jerusalem, and they were all scattered throughout the regions of Judea and Samaria, <u>except the apostles</u>. . . . Now those who were scattered went about preaching the word. Acts 8:1, 4 (emphasis added)*

Notice that when persecution hit the first Church, everyone left Jerusalem except the leaders. Those that were scattered went about preaching the Word. This means that the average believer learned how to share the Gospel. And the church grew.

If Jesus expects spiritual maturity, then practically, we must have ways of moving people from spiritual rebirth and infancy to becoming mature believers equipped to work in the harvest fields. Every believer. Not one, not some, not most, but we must aim to equip everyone. It's not a matter of whether we will be in the field, it is a matter of which one.

Know your field. There are multiple types of harvest fields:

- Geographical: centered on people where you live or will move to
- Needs-based: aimed at ministering to a felt-need through Jesus' love, such as sickness, poverty, grief, relational brokenness, or addiction
- Occupational: focused on your workplace or people of your specific occupation
- Educational: focused on a particular school
- Family: focused on bringing your family to faith in Jesus

These are just a few. The important thing is to ask the Lord of the harvest where He wants you. And then do it. Remember that different fields require different approaches and strategies. Begin to pray and believe that God will give you visions and dreams on how to reach the harvest field He has assigned you to.

Know your message. It is important that we are crystal clear on our message. It can be communicated in different ways but will emphasize the following:

- We were made by God.
- Sin has separated us from God and brought about spiritual death.
- God in His love came to bring us back to life and restore a relationship with Him.
- We must choose to turn from our ways back to God and follow Jesus as the Shepherd of our souls.

Know your abilities and gifts. Every ability or gift you have can be used as a sickle in the harvest field—a means to bring people face-to-face with God's love.

- If it's cooking, volunteer at a soup kitchen and tell people Jesus loves them.
- If it's leadership, lead initiatives for change in the harvest field, and then point people to Jesus.
- If it's serving, mow someone's grass, or meet another need, and tell them that Jesus loves them.
- If it's intercession and prayer, pray over your city and people you encounter. Join with evangelists to serve in their prayer and altar teams.

Know your co-laborers. It's important not to go it alone. As you approach your harvest field, consider the following:

- What other people or ministries are already working here? How can we work together? We should seek to form Kingdom alliances, joining ministries for effectiveness in the fields.
- Who are the people in my immediate church family? Do I just attend services with them, or am I truly connected with them for spiritual support, even as the original group of seventy (and more specifically twelve) disciples of Jesus were?
- Who should be my personal ministry partners? Jesus sent out His original disciples in pairs.[109]

ENDURING IMPENDING PERSECUTION

Most of our weekly church activity does very little to practically prepare the average persons to be mothers and fathers who can birth and care for the sons and daughters that will be born into the Kingdom through the great harvest. If we do not have harvesters in the field or systems to care for the harvest after it is harvested, it will rot. It will not stand the test of time or the winter of persecution.

Even now, to avoid persecution, compromise and silence from church leaders on critical areas are bringing a strong delusion and deception to the church. Tough times are coming to the true Church. Unless we begin to drastically change what we do, much of the coming harvest, and indeed many in the church now, will fall away and be eternally lost.

The global Covid-19 pandemic and ensuing challenges revealed that many, if not most, in the American church are not ready for hard times. People's faith faltered and failed after only a few weeks of an interrupted routine. The Lord kept saying to me during this time, "If people can't keep up with the foot soldiers, what will they do when they must keep up with the horsemen?"[110]

A bad attitude serves no good purpose. We must be able to do more than just complain. Jesus said to rejoice in persecution. "Take joy, for I have overcome the world" (John 16:33) Many things in the world will frustrate and even anger us, but we can't bring the authority of Christ into chaos when driven or tainted by anger, fear, accusation, or frustration.

Pointing out that the government is corrupt doesn't change it. If all nations will hate us for the sake of the Gospel, that means our nation as well.[111] It's inevitable. Simply pointing it out on social media or in conversations and arguing with those who disagree does not prepare us to endure hardship as a good soldier.

We must do more than lean on the arm of the flesh. Stockpiling weapons and food will not solve all hardship. We should be wise and live reasonably prepared for the future, but we may find ourselves in the middle of a whole multitude of problems we cannot avoid or adequately prepare for. So how will we get through? We must realize we are fighting a spiritual battle against spiritual enemies, not flesh and blood. We must learn to be led by the Spirit, not by the impulses of the flesh.

This is about more than one's view of the Great Tribulation. Often when you talk about the Church suffering in hard times, people dismiss it, because they say we will be raptured—taken away—before the Great Tribulation, or that the Great Tribulation is not coming to the world at all.

- Even if you believe we will not experience any part of the Great Tribulation, we must be prepared to endure hardship as a good soldier of the faith (2 Timothy 2:3-5).
- Jesus said, "In this world you will have trouble" (John 16:33).
- Jesus warned us that the conditions of His return would be tumultuous, and that all nations will turn against us for His name's sake (Matthew 24, especially v. 9).
- Jesus told us that the world will hate us because it hated Him (John 15:18).

Consider the millions of Christians in the world enduring hardship for the cause of Christ right now. Think about those in China. Iran. Afghanistan. We can't tell them the church will never endure hardship, because they are already in it.

You might not ever undergo persecution or imprisonment for your faith. But at some point in your life, you will endure some form of hardship. It could be times of deep pain, grief, or betrayal. Times when you're isolated and feel alone. Or times when you're going through prolonged illness and sickness.

If the Gospel we preach is only useful for escaping difficulty, what will we do when we experience it? How will we prepare our children to face it for the cause of Christ? What about our grandchildren? We must prepare and teach the next generations to stay prepared. If Christ delays His return, we must build a legacy that will be ready for Him and that season.

Most of the focus in our current churches will be useless during tough times. Most of what we call "ministry" is only roles we assume when the church gathers for weekend church. If the church can't gather, most of these roles have little or meaning. In other words, most of our ministry is useless during persecution.

Practically, we must change what we are doing. We must trim the fat, focus on what's important, and do it well. This is not a message against the need for the public gathering of the church. This is a message against spiritual immaturity. After all, mature Christians realize the value and power of true Christian community and will gather unless it becomes impossible to do so. But then what?

We must all grow up spiritually. Serious disciples of Jesus do not have the luxury of remaining immature. We can't wait until it starts raining to build an ark. We must act now, making these core changes:

- Broaden our definition of church as more than a weekly gathering with optional prayer meetings and Bible studies.
- Gain a larger view of ministry than just what is needed in people and giftings to pull off the weekly service and occasional fellowships.
- Redefine our expectations of church leadership and their roles.
- Develop a wider perspective on leadership (not to be confused with lowering our expectations).
- Release church leaders to fulfill their oversight roles.
- Alter our definition of a normal Christian.
- Help every believer take responsibility for sharing the Gospel and mentoring new believers.
- Create environments for all Christians to learn to care for and mentor others.
- Live with Jesus as the central focus of every aspect of our lives.

May we be committed to using every resource at our disposal to reach and train disciples of no one else but Jesus.

Only then can we truly experience a Jesus Revival.

Appendix 1: Integrating Prayer into the Life of the Church

APPENDICES

Appendix 1
Integrating Prayer into the Life of the Church

Ideas on returning corporate prayer to the church

Intentional times of prayer
- Create soaking spaces for extended times with God
- Host corporate prayer services that teach people how to pray
- Call regular times of focused intercession and day and night intercession

The weekly corporate worship service
- Engage in pre- and post-service prayer
- Give altar calls where people can come forward to seek salvation as well as freedom, healing, and deliverance
- Pray for the lost during services
- Offer weekly Communion for self-examination and repentance
- Dedicate the regular service completely to worship and intercession once every four to six weeks, with various prayer leaders focused on different areas of prayer (interwoven with worship)

Small group and church meetings
- Spend at least 25 percent of group meeting time in fervent prayer, using models that teach participants how to pray
- Begin business meetings with an extended time of prayer, before decisions are made

Appendix 1: Integrating Prayer into the Life of the Church

- Call the church into corporate prayer and fasting when leadership is being elected and appointed

From the suggestions given, list some practical ways that you can implementing prayer back into the life of your church:

Appendix 2
A Healthy Discipleship Plan

KEY COMPONENTS TO NURTURING HEALTHY DISCIPLES

Develop mentoring leaders. Mentoring will be a primary factor in the healthy growth of new Christians. Because of this, the personal character of leaders must be key—it must outweigh personal charisma or gifts. Leadership abilities can be taught to those who don't have them, but character is decided by the individual.
If it is overlooked, you'll have new disciples—baby Christians—remain immature and become lukewarm. They will not be able to withstand the winter that is surely going to come up on the church.

Leadership responsibilities can be tailored to match an individual's personal capacity to lead others—some can lead one or two, while others can lead larger groups.

Curriculum. The basic discipleship curriculum used is also significant. Choose a standard curriculum that all discipleship groups use. All new believers should complete the study with the help of a mentoring leader. It can serve as the hinge point of all future discipling in your church. Consider making it a prerequisite for membership, as this will give you and other leaders time to examine the lives of new believers coming into the church.

Good discipleship curriculum should teach new believers (among other things) to:

Appendix 2: A Healthy Discipleship Plan

- Study and interpret Scripture
- Pray
- Identify and overcome patterns of sin
- Resolve conflict
- Forgive
- Discover and use their spiritual gifts to build the church
- Share their faith and lead others to Christ
- Pray for others
- Disciple other believers
- Honor God with all of their resources

Growth in these areas will produce strong believers. Couple this training with a mentor who leads them to apply these things in real life scenarios, and you will form reproducing disciples. Create a plan for developing people to maturity and equipping them to care for new believers.

Visit www.discoverdiscipleship.com to access a comprehensive discipleship course that covers the above-mentioned skills. (Significant Church discounts are usually available)

HOW TO GET STARTED WITH DISCIPLING GROUPS

Train leaders first. All new leaders should first be mentored by someone themselves. Ideally the senior pastor and spouse would lead the first discipleship group, taking several potential leaders of both sexes through the material and coaching them into life practice. Perhaps you could start with your elders, deacons, Sunday School teachers, and chosen small group leaders.

It is common for current church leaders to resist going through personal discipleship. They will often be willing to lead others, but do not see the need to be led themselves. This can be particularly true the longer they have been in ministry.

Emphasize the fact that you are *all* learning new ways to implement relational discipleship together. Also, emphasize they will be setting an example by first experiencing the process they are asking others to engage in.

This will allow you to grow relationally with leaders who will be mentoring in the future. You will build a church family, as a church family. Most church leaders have not experienced a mentoring relationship with another believer. Moving through this process will give them an opportunity to experience what they will be leading others into. It will give you an opportunity to infuse the values and DNA into future groups. You will be intentionally investing into spiritual sons and daughters who will grow and invest in others.

Group makeup. Each new group should consist of a leader who has completed discipleship and leadership training, an apprentice leader who has completed a discipleship course and is in leadership training, and two to three new participants. The goal of these groups is not to see how big they can grow, but rather how many strong disciples, new leaders, and new groups they can form.

When to meet. Ideally, use one of the meeting times you already have on the weekly calendar. Adding another meeting to people's schedules will undermine the discipleship process.

Perhaps take your mid-week gathering and spend forty-five minutes to an hour in discipleship groups, followed by the same amount of time in corporate prayer. Offer a general Bible study for newcomers, those waiting to start discipleship, and those who have finished discipleship and are waiting to mentor others (one class for all).

Also consider turning adult and teen Sunday School classes into discipleship times. If you have a traditional setting with only one adult Sunday School teacher, they may need to flex a little. He or she would adopt a new role of supporting new group leaders. They could also teach a general Sunday School class for newcomers, those waiting to start discipleship, and those who have finished discipleship and are waiting to mentor others.

If you meet during Sunday School or other larger group times, three to four smaller breakout groups could meet in the church sanctuary, with more in the fellowship hall. (For example, three to four men's groups could meet in one place, and three to four women's groups could meet in the other.)

By doing these things, you will create a safe environment for people to learn how to lead, as well as many strong Christians who can care for new believers. Twenty-five people in your church could, within a few months, mature to the point of caring for 100–125 new believers.

Leadership support. Make sure there is regular (at least monthly) time to support and care for the group leaders. Place a church elder or deacon over three to four group leaders and the people they lead. Have them pray for those people regularly and provide support for the leaders.

Jesus Revival

Endnotes

Chapter 1

1 Keith J. Hardman, Charles Grandison Finney: 1792-1875 (Grand Rapids: Baker Book House, 1987), 9, in Patrick Morely, "A Brief History of Revival and Awakening in America," Church Leaders, August 23, 2021, accessed May 14, 2020, https://churchleaders.com/outreach-missions/outreach-missions-articles/257668-brief-history-spiritual-revival-awakening-america.html.

2 Patrick Morely, "A Brief History of Revival and Awakening in America," Church Leaders, August 23, 2021, accessed May 14, 2020, https://churchleaders.com/outreach-missions/outreach-missions-articles/257668-brief-history-spiritual-revival-awakening-america.html

3 Merriam-Webster, s.v. "revive," https://www.merriam-webster.com/dictionary/revive.

4 Duncan Campbell, The Price and Power of Revival (Solid Christian Books, 2015), pp. 45-46

5 Campbell, Revival, p.47

6 This was taken from the testimony of Steve Seamands in the "Night of Prayer and Remembering," When God Comes: Celebrating the 50th Anniversary: 1070 Asbury Revival, in Hughes Auditorium at Asbury University, Wilmore, KY, February 2, 2020.

7 Psalm 85:6.

8 Matthew 13:44-46.

9 Leonard Sweet and Frank Viola, Jesus Manifesto: Restoring the Supremacy and Sovereignty of Jesus Christ, (Nashville, TN: Thomas Nelson, 2010).

Chapter 2

10 Acts 2:12.

Chapter 3

11 Daniel K. Norris, "It Was the Call to Revival That Awakened a Nation," Trail of Fire (blog), Trail of Fire, accessed May 14, 2020, http://trailoffire.org/fireblog/it-was-the-sound-of-revival-that-awakened-a-nation/.

12 John Burton, "It's Time to Start Scaring Visitors Away From Our Churches," Burton.tv, August 23, 2018, accessed May 14, 2020, https://burton.tv/2018/08/23/its-time-to-start-scaring-visitors-away-from-our-churches/.

13 Duncan Campbell, The Price and Power of Revival (Solid Christian Books, 2015), p. 43.

14 Rick Joyner, The World on Fire: The Welsh Revival and Its Lessons for Our Times (MorningStar Publications, Dec. 5, 2013).

15 Luke 22:42 (my paraphrase).

Endnotes

16 Blue Letter Bible, s.v. "kathizo (tarry)," Strong's Concordance, G2523, in "Transliteration" and Larry Pierce, "Outline of Biblical Usage," accessed date January 10, 2022, https://www.blueletterbible.org/lexicon/g2523/kjv/tr/0-1/.

17 Matthew 18:20.

18 Luke 24:49; Acts 1:8.

19 Acts 12:5-7.

20 Acts 16:25-16.

21 Edward Langton, History of the Moravian Church; The Story of the First International Protestant Church (London: Allen & Unwin, 1956)

22 Dan Graves, "Jeremy Lanphier Led Prayer Revival," Christianity.com, May 3, 2010, https://www.christianity.com/church/church-history/timeline/1801-1900/jeremy-lanphier-led-prayer-revival-11630507.html.

23 Mark Galli, "Revival at Cane Ridge," in "Camp Meetings & Circuit Riders: Frontier Revivals," Christianity Today, Issue 45, 1995, https://www.christianitytoday.com/history/issues/issue-45/revival-at-cane-ridge.html.

24 Truth In History, "The Welsh Revival of 1904-1905," accessed February 10, 2019, http://truthinhistory.org/the-welsh-revival-of-1904-1905-2.html.

25 David Smithers, ed. and comp., "The Intercessors of the Hebrides Revival," Call the Nation to Prayer, accessed January 10, 2022, https://ctntp.uk/other-insights/the-intercessors-of-the-hebrides-revival/.

26 Matthew 26:40.

27 The Jesus Gathering, "Charles Finney, January 10. 2022 ??, https://www.thejesusgathering.org/charles-finney.html.

28 Campbell, Revival, pp. 43-44.

29 Matthew 1:21.

30 2 Corinthians 5:17.

31 John 16:8.

Chapter 4

32 Blue Letter Bible, ESV, s.v., G3340 in Thayer's Greek Lexicon, accessed January 10, 2022, https://www.blueletterbible.org/lexicon/g3340/esv/mgnt/0-1/.

33 James 2:19.

34 1 John 3:8.

35 Galatians 5:15-16.

36 Tim Barnett, "Is It Unloving to Tell People They Are Sinners?" Stand To Reason, December 20, 2015, https://www.str.org/blog/is-it-unloving-to-tell-people-they-are-sinners#.XQQ03y2ZPOQ.

37 C. S. Lewis, The Problem of Pain (London: HarperCollins, 2012).

38 Matthew 5:11-12.

39 Matthew 11:28-30.

40 Ray Comfort, "Hell's Best Kept Secret," Living Waters, July 27, 2019, https://www.livingwaters.com/hells-best-kept-secret/.

41 Matthew 13:44.

42 Justin Taylor, "He Was No Fool," The Gospel Coalition (blog), January 9, 2010, https://www.thegospelcoalition.org/blogs/justin-taylor/he-ws-no-fool/.

43 1 Peter 2:12 NLT.

44 Acts 5:41.

Chapter 5

45 This is adapted from the Westminster Shorter Catechism, developed in 1646-1647. A catechism is a summary of Christian doctrines, taught in question-and-answer format. Refer here: http://www.shortercatechism.com/resources/wsc/ wsc_001.html.

46 David Platt, Because We Are Called to Counter Culture: In a World of Poverty, Same-Sex Marriage, Racism, Sex Slavery, Immigration, Persecution, Abortion, Orphans, and Pornography, (Carol Stream, IL: Tyndale House, 2015).

47 Bill Hull, The Complete Book of Discipleship: On Being and Making Followers of Christ, (Colorado Springs, CO: NavPress, 2006).

48 Wikipedia, s.v. "discipleship (Christianity)," last edited November 28, 2021, accessed February, 2021, https://en.wikipedia.org/wiki/Disciple_(Christianity)#cite_note-10.

49 1 John 2:6.

50 Acts 9:2; 22:4.

51 Thomas Jackson, ed., "The Sermons of John Wesley—Sermon 1: Salvation by Faith," in "Thomas Jackson's Numbering, Wesley Center Online, wesley.nnu.edu. http://wesley.nnu.edu/john-wesley/the-sermons-of-john-wesley-1872-edition/sermon-1-salvation-by-faith.

52 Romans 10:9-10.

Chapter 6

53 Michael Brown, "Stripper-Dancing Pastor Wives and Non-Judgmental Christianity" The Christian Post October 20, 2015, https://www.christianpost.com/news/stripper-dancing-pastor-wives-non-judgmental-christianity.html

54 Matthew 28:18-20.

55 2 Corinthians 13:5.

Endnotes

56 Greg L. Hawkins and Cally Parkinson, Move: What 1,000 Churches Reveal about Spiritual Growth (Grand Rapids, MI: Zondervan, 2011).

57 2 Corinthians 5:21.

58 Isaiah 53:6.

59 2 Corinthians 7:10.

60 Hebrews 10:29.

61 Leonard Sweet and Frank Viola, Jesus Manifesto: Restoring the Supremacy and Sovereignty of Jesus Christ (Nashville, TN: Thomas Nelson, 2010), locs. 550-553, Kindle.

62 Galatians 5:22-23.

63 Merriam-Webster, s.v. "judge," accessed date?, https://www.merriam-webster.com/dictionary/judge.

64 James F. White, Documents of Christian Worship: Descriptive and Interpretive Sources, (Louisville, KY: Westminster/John Knox Press, 1992), locs. 695-697, Kindle.

65 Matthew 7:1-5.

66 Galatians 6:1.

67 Matthew 7:15.

Chapter 7

68 Matthew 18:20.

69 Francis Chan, Forgotten God: Reversing Our Tragic Neglect of the Holy Spirit, (Colorado Springs, CO: David C. Cook, 2009), p. 90.

70 Leonard Sweet and Frank Viola, Jesus Manifesto: Restoring the Supremacy and Sovereignty of Jesus Christ (Nashville, TN: Thomas Nelson, 2010), locs. 540-544, Kindle.

71 This refers to the words of Christ printed in red in many Bibles.

72 Leonard Sweet and Frank Viola, Jesus Manifesto: Restoring the Supremacy and Sovereignty of Jesus Christ (Nashville, TN: Thomas Nelson, 2010), locs., 1490-1496, Kindle.

Chapter 9

73 1 John 4:19.

74 Mark 12:30-31.

75 Matthew 25:40-45.

76 Matthew 28:18-20; 2 Corinthians 5:19.

77 This quote has been attributed to St. Francis of Assisi. However, as the following article explains, there is no record that he ever said this. St. Francis actually preached, with words, wherever he went. In Kevin Cotter, "Did Francis Really Say, "Preach the Gospel at All times and If Necessary. Use Words?" Focus,

October 4, 2011, https://focusoncampus. org/content/did-francis-really-say-preach-the-gospel-at-all-times-and-if-nec-essary-use-words.

78 Larry Pierce, "Outline of Biblical Usage (II.)", Blue Letter Bible, s.v. "kerysso (preach)," accessed January 2022 https://www.blueletterbible.org/lang/lexicon/lexi- con.cfm?Strongs=G2784&t=KJV.

79 2 Timothy 4:5.

Chapter 10

80 John 12:2.

81 Luke 10:38–42, Luke 9:60.

82 Luke 4:16–29.

83 Oxford English Dictionary Online, s.v. "communion," Lexico, accessed date??, https://www.lexico.com/en/communion.

84 Blue Letter Bible, s.v. "kathizo (tarry)," Strong's Concordance, G2523, in "Transliteration" and Larry Pierce, "Outline of Biblical Usage," accessed date January 10, 2022, https://www.blueletterbible.org/lexicon/g2523/kjv/tr/0-1/.

85 Matthew 5:1–2.

86 Matthew 26:38, 40.

87 Blue Letter Bible, s.v. "baptizo (baptize)," Strong's Concordance, G907, accessed date January 10, 2022 https://www.blueletterbible.org/lexicon/g907/kjv/tr/0-1/.

88 John 21:1–19.

89 2 Corinthians 8:1–5.

90 Matthew 11:28–30.

91 John Bevere, "Good or God?"

92 Reference Acts 16:6–10 for an example.

93 Psalm 127:1.

94 Psalms 23.

Chapter 11

95 1 Samuel 17.

96 Page C-08, The Cell En-CELL-clopedia A Comprehensive Cell Resource, Twyla Brickman Strategic Cell Ministries International Nairobi, Kenya.

Chapter 14

97 2 Timothy 4:3.

Endnotes

98 Matthew 11:6.

99 Acts 2:12.

100 1 Corinthians 1:21.

101 Greg L. Hawkins and Cally Parkinson, Move: What 1,000 Churches Reveal about Spiritual Growth (Grand Rapids, MI: Zondervan, 2011)

Chapter 15

102 John Bevere, "A Good Reputation Isn't Enough," Facebook video, Colorado Springs, CO, December 5, 2015, https://www.facebook.com/JohnBevere.page/videos/10153790912318011.

103 New Living Translation

104 Luke 18:1-8

105 Duncan Campbell, The Price and Power of Revival (Solid Christian Books, 2015), p. 43

106 Revelations 3:15

Chapter 16

107 Jeremiah 12:5

108 Luke 19:13

109 Luke 10:1; Mark 6:7

110 Jeremiah 12:5

111 Matthew 24:9

Made in the USA
Middletown, DE
17 September 2024